there is nothing to fear

FROM BREAKDOWN TO ENLIGHTENMENT

HEATHER BINNS

First published by Ultimate World Publishing 2022
Copyright © 2022 Heather Binns

ISBN

Paperback: 978-1-922714-79-4
Ebook: 978-1-922714-80-0

Heather Binns has asserted her rights under the Copyright, Designs and Patents Act 1988 to be identified as the author of this work. The information in this book is based on the author's experiences and opinions. The publisher specifically disclaims responsibility for any adverse consequences which may result from use of the information contained herein. Permission to use information has been sought by the author. Any breaches will be rectified in further editions of the book.

All rights reserved. No part of this publication may be reproduced, stored in or introduced into a retrieval system, or transmitted in any form, or by any means (electronic, mechanical, photocopying, recording or otherwise) without the prior written permission of the author. Any person who does any unauthorised act in relation to this publication may be liable to criminal prosecution and civil claims for damages. Enquiries should be made through the publisher.

Cover design: Ultimate World Publishing
Layout and typesetting: Ultimate World Publishing
Editor: Emily Riches
Cover photo copyright licence: LedyX-Shutterstock.com

Ultimate World Publishing
Diamond Creek,
Victoria Australia 3089
www.writeabook.com.au

Acknowledgement Of Country

I acknowledge the traditional custodians of this land on which I live, the Gumbaynggirr people. I recognise their long history on this land and the care they have given to it for thousands of years.

I would like to pay my respects to the Elders past, present and emerging, and thank them for allowing me to both live and write this book on their land.

Book Reviews

'Heather is a natural storyteller and I was completely captivated by the story of her breakdown and brave journey to healing. Her drive to share this story with others, so they too can learn and grow from it, is a real gift. Writing as a tool for healing and growth is clearly of the utmost importance in her life (along with horses!), and this really shines out from the page. I'm sure all her readers will find this book both inspiring and empowering.'

Emily Riches
Editor

'*There is Nothing to Fear* is a courageous memoir that is difficult to put down. Heather has an ability to draw you in, and transport you into her worlds: past, present, future and every timeline in between. Every chapter includes a helpful summary and tips for the reader, and Heather so skilfully describes the deep desire that we all have: to belong, to be seen, and to be unconditionally loved and appreciated. A stunning book with a lot of soul.'

Yelena Fishman
Psychologist
Author of *What's Normal Anyway? The keys to unlocking your mental well-being.*

'A few times in our lives we experience life changing moments. This is a great recounting of how one such event came about. This is evidence that you can come out the other side stronger, if you are willing to work hard and face all the pains that came before.'

Dr. Isobel Roberts

• ● •

'Heather Binns is the strongest, most compassionate woman I have ever known. I first met Heather in a carpark preparing for an Adventure Girls 'learn to surf' session. I was nervous and she was able to settle me with a few kind words... We have been friends and partners in all things 'mindful' for over 20 years.

Her book is not only powerful, it is also practical. Heather shows you how to face your fears and live an authentic life. She gives great insight on self-expression and the importance of following your joy. I highly recommend this book and know your life will benefit on all levels.'

Sheryl Duguid
Pure Heart Wellbeing

• ● •

'Can there be any more important pursuit for the mature thinker than fathoming the heights and depths of our existence – the meaning of life, the universe and everything?

I have known Heather since 1977, where, in our beloved bushwalkers' club, she and her sisters provided the down-to-earth balance and the essential social spice to make those years among the most favourite of this particular lifetime for so many of us!

Thanks, Heather, for filling in the gaps in our knowledge and awareness of your amazing journey and embarking on inspiring others with your precious experience. *"No mud – no lotus!"* ~ *Thich Nhat Hanh.*'

Chris Gillen

•●•

'Heather's book is an honest and open recount of her life's happenings. Her ability to move through the challenges in her life and not remain in a victim mindset is truly inspirational!'

Coral Brian Wheatley,
Author of *Building Wealth in a*
Self-Managed Super Fund

•●•

'Since first meeting Heather online through her blog (and many postings), she has impressed me hugely with her honesty and willingness to share her experiences. It has been fascinating to follow her story and so inspirational to read how she has overcome many hardships and setbacks along the way. I am looking forward to reading her book in its entirety. A sneak peek has shown me that this is a story which will bring hope, comfort and inspiration to the many normal people who find themselves in depression and despair and are searching for answers. Wishing Heather every success with this valuable book.'

Dr. Mary Concannon, BSc
Lecturer, Speaker, Animal Behaviourist

Dedication

To my parents Betty and Richard – I miss you.

To my sisters Ros and Sue, who travelled much of this journey with me.

To my husband Doug, who has supported me all the way.

To my children Matt and Emma, my greatest achievements in life.

To my half-sister Liz, a wonderful surprise, and missing piece of the puzzle!

Contents

Acknowledgement Of Country	iii
Book Reviews	v
Dedication	ix
Foreword	1
Introduction	3
Chapter One: The Breakdown	7
Chapter Two: Entering The Tunnel	23
Chapter Three: Finding Kindness And Love	35
Chapter Four: Meeting The Child Within	51
Chapter Five: Darkness In The Sun	65
Chapter Six: My World Crashes Down	87
Chapter Seven: The Darkest Days Of All	107
Chapter Eight: The Invisible Girl	123
Chapter Nine: Change Creates Chaos	141
Chapter Ten: It's All An Illusion!	159
Chapter Eleven: It Was Always About The Horses	171
Chapter Twelve: Following The Dream	187
Chapter Thirteen: The Remembering	203
Afterword	223
About The Author	225
Book Reviews From The Family	229
Speaker Bio	231
Acknowledgements	233

Foreword

'...and the day came when the risk to remain tight in a bud was more painful than the risk it took to blossom.'

— Anais Nin

There is Nothing to Fear is a wonderful account of one courageous woman's journey into her inner world.

Heather came to therapy in January 2000 when she was experiencing what she described as a breakdown, only to discover it was the breakthrough her life needed. Heather was open to exploring a way of therapy based on John Bradshaw's book, *Homecoming*, that involved going back to the beginning of her life and reclaiming the inner child who became wounded from early experiences, at each of the developmental stages of psychosocial development. Heather was to discover that it wasn't easy and, as she explored her past experiences, she would find herself at times grief-stricken, sad, amazed, happy, angry, amused, bemused, fascinated, dumbfounded and so much more.

Heather was deeply committed to her personal work and recovery and courageously followed her feelings where they needed to go. Heather attended regular therapy sessions, as well as being actively engaged in journal writing, regular meditation and remaining open and curious to new experiences that occurred. As Heather explored, digested and integrated her past experiences, her world opened up in ways she never imagined. Heather realised that this journey was more than just a way to manage her anxiety and depression: it was a catalyst to a new way of being in the world and for her, it was a spiritual awakening.

It was an honour to be part of Heather's journey. It was an honour to witness the profound emergence and symmetry of such beautiful discoveries in her life. It is hoped this book will be helpful to others with Heather's honest and open account of her experiences as well as the inclusion of her learnings and tips for the readers at the end of each chapter.

And hopefully this book will encourage others to be willing to step into the world of inner personal work which is the most important work we have to do, for ourselves and for the world.

Jannelle Geraghty
Psychologist
2021

Introduction

Welcome to my story! I suggest that you make yourself a cup of tea, then settle somewhere comfy to read. Take your time to fully immerse yourself in the magical world I found myself in.

I use the word 'magical' even though much of this experience was painful because the pain of the journey led me to an unseen world.

This is the story of my breakdown which happened over 20 years ago, and how a wonderful psychologist and the power of writing led me to not only discover a long-buried passion, but also opened my eyes to the spiritual world and the wonders of the universe.

I travelled back to the beginning of my life to find the missing pieces of myself, and during that journey I learnt more than I could have ever imagined. I learnt about the power of love, the connected world and how so many of our answers lie within.

If you are struggling with meaning in life, feeling down and broken, feeling lonely and lost – or you would just like to read an interesting story, this book is for you! Each chapter includes important lessons I learnt, and notes for the reader. I suggest you read the story first, then go back and look at the lessons in depth.

I want to give you hope, and I want you to know that you are never alone.

You may want to delve as deep into your life as I did – or take some of the suggestions I make and use them to help navigate the world you live in.

I first knew I needed to write a book when I was going through the therapy. I began conversing with my child self through writing, which led to so much more! I knew then that what I was experiencing needed to be shared.

But why did it take me 20 years?

I had kept all my precious journals from that time carefully tucked away. When we experienced threats from bushfires in late 2019, the first item I packed was my box of journals. They were placed in my car with other precious items. In that situation, it's amazing to realise how little is of real value in our homes. We pack the treasured memories, the important documents, the pets… everything else is just embellishment to our lives!

We were fortunate that a wind change saved our district, but the boxes stayed packed and were all placed in our spare room. They were stacked on top of each other and stayed that way the following year.

Of course, 2020 was the year of COVID-19 – and it was also the year of a series of eye surgeries for me. I didn't bounce back well and suffered some complications. This led to post-surgery depression which plagued me over the Australian summer – but through all of this, I had the urge to find my journals, so I started sorting the boxes that were still quietly stacked in our spare room.

The box of journals was at the very bottom of the stack! I finally retrieved them and put them in the drawer under my bed. I was happy they were close to me – but what was I going to do? Why did I need them close?

I knew the words in them would help to form my book, but while I wanted them close by, I still didn't have the urge to actually start writing! That urge would happen in June 2021.

I am part of a local horse group, and I was holding an animal communication weekend (yes, I talk to horses)! The horses revealed some important messages – and I knew I had to start writing. But before I wrote a book about the horses, I needed to write this book, because this was the start of everything.

So now it is written – and yes, I have another book on the way! But first, settle back and read my story. My wish is that you find information that will help you.

Just remember – there is nothing to fear!

A WORD OF CAUTION

This book does not replace professional help. If you are struggling, please seek both medical and psychological help. I am a firm believer in both – but I am also a believer in so much more!

Chapter One

The Breakdown

> *'It is the client who knows what hurts, what directions to go, what problems are crucial, what experiences have been deeply buried.'*
>
> — Carl Rogers

It was late 1999. Here we were, almost at the turn of the century and what an exciting time it should have been – but I certainly wasn't partying like it was 1999. Instead, I found myself in the corner of my bedroom, on the floor, curled up into a little ball. The world was crashing in on me; it was all too hard. I'd tried to hold everything together for so long – now it felt like a metal blanket was descending over me.

I couldn't push it away any longer. 'You win,' I thought. I imagined that's how a prey animal feels as it's giving up the fight for life. I was crying and shaking, waiting for the end… The metal blanket enveloped me. I lay still, hardly able to breathe and stared at the same spot on the carpet for what seemed like an eternity.

Staying still helped. I couldn't move anyway as I seemed to be frozen, and my brain had become a blank screen. I was alone in the house, and that was a good thing. I didn't need the family to see me like this.

I whispered through my tears, 'Help me, please help me.'

How had my life come to this? Why had my body and mind shut down?

It felt safe in that corner, curled up on the floor... My bedroom was the best room in the house as far as I was concerned. Our family had lived in this house for three years – a house that was to be our forever home – but it wasn't a home. There was something weird and creepy about it and I only felt comfortable in the bedroom.

I knew I'd hit a brick wall. My body and mind had gone on strike. I had been in such a state of anxiety previously, and now anxiety's evil twin, depression, was joining in on the cycle...

Here I was at 43 years old, a wife and mother of two children, seemingly broken. How was I going to mend myself? I didn't want to die, and I felt like I could. I needed help – I knew I couldn't do it alone.

Let's now backtrack a couple of years to see what led to this event...

For several years I had been studying social science as a mature age student. My major was counselling, which I had completed, and I had just finished up the mediation courses through the School of Law. I had done very well, and I was never satisfied just to get a pass – it had to be a credit or more! However, in striving for excellence I had become a nervous wreck.

In June of 1999, I started to have anxiety attacks. I would spread my books out to work on the next assignment and start shaking, so I would put them away again and just sit on the bed. My body was doing strange things – I ended up with terrible cramping in my lower back to the point where the pain could be unbearable. My digestive system was a mess and my head and neck ached constantly.

I sought help. First, it was off to the doctor for a series of tests to find the cause of the aching. Was it bowel, back, urinary infection, kidney stones – or something else? All tests came back clear but they did note I'd had glandular fever.

'Ahh! You have chronic fatigue!' the doctor said. 'You need to rest and will need more sleep.'

'Okay,' I thought. 'I'd better cut down the number of units I'm studying each semester.' That was my answer to my troubles, but each time I got my books out to study, I shook. I tried to ignore the shaking, but then I realised I could not retain what I was reading. The words became jumbled, the assignment task just didn't make sense... Why couldn't I focus?

I decided to drive to the university to talk to the teaching staff, but as I got closer to my destination, I felt ill and started shaking. I ended up turning around and driving back home. Now, this was serious. I needed to change something, so I made a decision. I would defer my course until the following year, which was to be my final year. I had already completed more units than I needed to, so I would be able to slot these ones in and still graduate at the end of the year.

My aim was, once graduated, to work part time as a counsellor, with the possibility of doing more study to become a psychologist.

When my children were babies, I completed 12 months of study to be a Nursing Mothers' Counsellor. Looking back, I don't really know how I did it! Most of the study was completed at night once the children were in bed. I enjoyed running groups and exploring topics which new mothers really needed to talk about. I learnt a lot about group dynamics during that time and was quite fascinated by how to monitor everyone in a group so that they all felt comfortable. At the time, my plan was to eventually work for an organisation that ran groups – maybe for abused women, or for people with particular issues.

As I was relatively new to Coffs Harbour, I had also started a group called Adventure Girls. It was for women aged 30 to 80 who wanted to meet people and share fun adventures such as snorkelling, horse-riding, walking or the adventure of a night out or coffee morning etc. This group was in its infancy, but there had been a huge response. All this was happening at the same time I was experiencing the anxiety/depression cycle. However, in no time at all we had a core group – and it ended up being one of the best things I have ever done!

●●●

Now, back to the ailments I had been experiencing before I ended up in the foetal position in my bedroom...

Once I had decided to defer my course, I thought I would be back to normal in no time. This didn't happen. The lower back cramps were as bad as ever and I had the strangest feeling of fullness in my lower half. I finally came across someone who was recommended to me...

Enter Arthur, an ex-doctor and gymnast who was a Master in Zen Shiatsu. How fortunate he lived close by in the Coffs Harbour area. I visited Arthur many times, and he always had words of wisdom for me – as well as the most amazing acupressure sessions. After one session, the cramping eased – and after two sessions, it disappeared. It was wonderful to be free of pain.

Arthur would give me sayings each time and the one that he repeated over and over to me was this: **'If you try, you cry and die – relax and enjoy!'** I would nod in agreement, but I didn't really get it... until I did...

> 'If you try, you cry and die – relax and enjoy!'

All my life, I had TRIED. I had to be good and work hard. The trying was like working against something – everything had become hard and stressful – and most tasks were done with the thread of anxiety running through them. No wonder I was exhausted!

I didn't want to die, so I made the decision to defer my university course for the next 18 months. At the time, I thought that decision would solve all my problems!

During this time, we had family visitors which I often found stressful, and indeed, the cramping came back, so I returned to Arthur.

I received a lecture: 'Do you understand – these people are killing you! Just say NO!' I told him I couldn't do that. He replied, 'So you forsake yourself so as not to make waves? Aren't you worth more than that?'

I feebly responded that I hadn't thought of that. I just thought it was something I had to suffer…

Over the next few visits to Arthur, something different happened. During the acupressure, I had the feeling of 'something' moving up from my centre, to sit just behind my eyes. I didn't really know what it was… But I was about to find out!

•●•

So, let's now return to the November of 1999, with me curled up in the corner.

I knew that the 'something' that had moved during the session with Arthur had finally exploded out – sounds like the scene out of the *Alien* movie!

As I lay staring at the carpet, an awareness came to me. The way I viewed life, the way I lived in the world was somehow wrong. I realised that my whole life up to that point had been lived in a veil of depression. This didn't mean I had walked around full of misery – in fact I was probably too cheery! Even in happy times, my being was tainted with depression. I was seen as a positive, happy person... but I was depressed. And it had been that way my whole life. Yes, my whole life...

And I had not realised... until that very moment... staring at the carpet.

I felt sad and cheated. Why had I lived like that? When I could finally move, I grabbed a pen and paper, as I needed to draw it. It had been there since birth.

I drew this – **THE PIT OF DEPRESSION.**

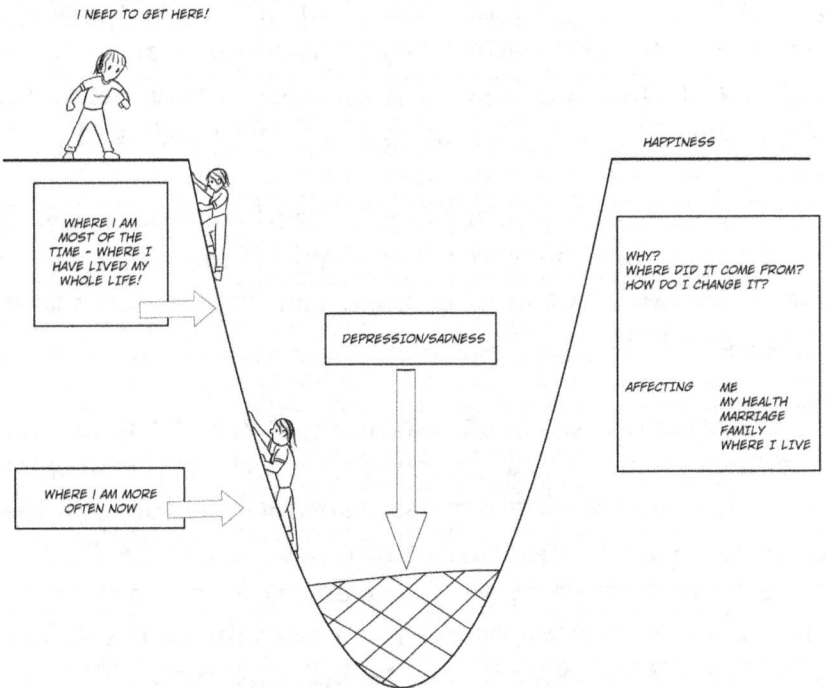

Sometimes, I was way down in the pit – and sometimes I had crawled to the top – but I had never crawled out! In fact, I was drawing chronic depression.

•●•

I knew what I needed to do: I needed to go back to the very beginning of my life and go through each step. I had to find out what had caused it. I needed to find a professional to help me – and I needed to start as soon as possible.

My neighbour knew some psychologists and gave me two names – I rang the first one and made an appointment. In the meantime, I still had an appointment with Arthur. I told him what had happened, and he immediately jumped up and danced around the room saying, 'Thank you guides! She's got it!' I couldn't understand why he was so delighted! He said, 'I could feel that in you from the start – I'm so happy you can see it. When you get these trivial bits sorted out you will be fine – a new person – you wait and see!'

As he was retiring from his work and moving away, he also said, 'If you need me, just think of me and I will be there.' Those words were of great comfort, as many times I did need him.

The day had come for the psychologist visit, about a week after my realisation had hit me. It had been a difficult week. I had been wandering aimlessly around the house in that time. I observed myself in the mirror – I looked odd – my eyes were glazed, and I looked not quite there. I had previously seen that look in a friend, who had a breakdown after buried memories resurfaced regarding childhood abuse. I called it 'The Breakdown Look.'

So I went to the psychologist, complete with 'The Breakdown Look' and proudly carrying my drawing of 'The Pit of Depression.' I was so relieved to be talking to someone about it. I repeated what had happened, talked about my realisation and proudly showed her my drawing.

However, she wasn't impressed. She dismissed how I felt and told me I had issues from my teenage years because my mother prevented me from going out and doing normal teenage things. I shook my head to say I didn't think that was the problem. She told me I needed to buy a book called *Beating the Blues* and do the exercises suggested. I felt a mixture of relief and confusion as I left. I made an appointment for two weeks' time and left to go and find this book.

My husband, Doug, asked me how it went when he got home. I said I was relieved to talk about it – but something felt wrong. As I looked at the recommended book, I saw it had good suggestions for helping with depression, but it didn't address what was important to me. At that point, I didn't want band-aid solutions. I wanted to go back to the past and unravel the mystery of the lifelong depression.

Over the next few days, I felt angry, which was a nice change from feeling depressed! I started to analyse the session I'd had with the psychologist. Because I had knowledge in counselling, I realised she had broken some of the most basic rules and had decided herself what my problem was rather than guiding me through the process. She had also self-disclosed about her time as a teenager, deciding my problems were the same as hers. One of the golden rules of counselling is never to self-disclose

– only when there is good rapport with the client and if the situation calls for it.

I was very thankful for my counselling knowledge. When you are so vulnerable, you aren't really in the right frame of mind to shop around for the best help. Having that knowledge was one of the best things that came from my university study!

I rang to cancel the next appointment with her – I didn't need to go back.

I had previously told my mother I wasn't well and was going to see a psychologist. I heard the shock in her voice. She wasn't comfortable with these things, even though she had seen a psychiatrist herself many years previously – and she certainly wasn't comfortable that I was visiting a psychologist. Mum had always been wonderful to me when my children were young. In fact, you could say she was very generous with help – with the 'doing' – but not so good when it came to emotional support.

She said to me, 'Oh Heather, you don't need to see a psychologist! It's just something we have to live with – I've been depressed all my life!'

I thought to myself, 'And this is why I need mental help!'

When I next spoke to Mum, I told her that the psychologist had given me a book, but I wasn't going to see her again. I felt her relief! She said to me, 'Yes, you will be fine, you don't need to see her!'

I decided then that I wouldn't mention my depression to her again, and she never asked me how I was doing after

The Breakdown

that. In fact, I was very careful who I mentioned it to. I didn't need anyone to put doubts in my mind of what I needed to do – I was an emotional wreck, so I knew I was vulnerable.

It was now almost Christmas. I wondered if I could see the second psychologist on my list before the holiday season. I rang to make an appointment and sadly, I would have to wait until after New Year.

Christmas was a struggle. I had always put a lot of effort in for the kids, but this year it was hard. Fortunately, we were on our own. Mum was heading to Sydney to be with my sister and her very young children, and Doug's family were staying in Sydney. Phew! For many years, Christmas had been at our place with all the family coming to us. At least this year we could be on our own.

I spent those weeks feeling like I could hardly move – like I was walking through sticky mud. I stayed on my bed when I could, did what I needed to do for my kids and generally wallowed in depression.

Finally, it was time for my appointment with the second psychologist. I thought I was going to burst! I sat down in Jannelle's office and proceeded to tell her that I was having some sort of breakdown. She responded by saying, 'How wonderful! From a crisis comes change! Now you will save yourself from illness if you can let go of what has been bottled up inside!' I was amazed she could think it was wonderful – I just wanted to get out of the state I was in!

So, through my sobs, I told my story, and I once again showed my drawing of The Pit of Depression. Rather than dismissing the drawing, she nodded in understanding! Afterwards, Jannelle summed up the session and agreed that we needed to go back to the beginning. She assured me that it was a wonderful thing that was happening, and if I was prepared to work through it, my life would change enormously – in a good way!

She asked me if I had read the book *Homecoming* by John Bradshaw, as she thought that was a good book to work with. I borrowed her copy until I could buy my own, and my homework was to start at the beginning of my life and write down all the facts I knew about that time.

I wondered how that would help – I certainly didn't remember much as a baby and small child. I could write details of where we lived etc. but how would that help? Jannelle replied, 'Your feelings will tell the story.'

I left that session feeling such a huge sense of relief as I had been listened to and understood. This was exactly what I needed! I drove home full of hope. Maybe there was a way out of the quicksand that I found myself in.

•●•

MY LEARNINGS

- If I didn't get help, I could die.

- My anxiety came from trying to be perfect.

- I realised that I had been depressed all my life.

- One of the best outcomes from my time studying social science was the fact that I could recognise when I needed to find another psychologist who understood me.

- I learnt to be careful with who I told of my struggles, to avoid outside influence.

FOR THE READER

- Don't struggle alone if you are depressed or anxious. See your doctor or psychologist – or both.

- Depression is a broad area. You may fix yourself with a few helpful suggestions, or you may need much more in-depth help.

- I needed to go back to the beginning of my life – that was my starting point – but it may not be yours. Search for a professional who can truly understand what you are conveying.

- Choose wisely who you confide in if you are struggling. Not all will understand – in fact, not many at all will understand. Find the best support you can!

Chapter Two
Entering The Tunnel

'Feeling empty is a form of chronic depression, as one is perpetually in mourning for one's true self.'

— **John Bradshaw**

'To find yourself, you need to lose yourself.'

— **Heather Binns**

When I arrived home, I jumped on my bed and started reading the book, *Homecoming*. I couldn't believe it! Had he written this book for me? He used terms like wounded child, wonder child and inner child. All these terms would have been dismissed by me at any other time in my life – but in the days, weeks, months and years of my own emotional crisis, it all made perfect sense.

So, this was the 'thing' I had felt behind my eyes. It was my real self, struggling to get out! I could say that Arthur awakened that child within. It was now time for her to be heard.

The first part of John Bradshaw's book discusses how your inner child became wounded. There were parts in the book that related to my crisis, particularly about the feelings of depression and emptiness. He explains that we are depressed because our true self is never present. We can feel like we are forever standing observing life, rather than being truly in it, because we are not comfortable in our own skin. We may feel a yearning – yet we don't know what we are yearning for. The truth is we are yearning for our real self.

'Oh! There it is!' I thought. Tears were falling: 'Someone understands! He knows!' I was sitting on the bed cross-legged, rocking back and forth.

Someone understood!

I had always felt like I was running to catch up, like I lived on an invisible perimeter – on the outskirts of life. I was never IN life!

I had a family, I had friends, but I often felt alone – like I wasn't part of anything. I could pretend, even though I wasn't aware I was pretending. I could be cheery and seem confident but really, I was just terrified of the world! I felt 'lesser.' In my eyes, everyone else seemed to be part of something: they belonged and I didn't. I had always thought that it was just my lot in life.

The only way I could be worthy was to do an excellent job and be extremely responsible and sensible. I was very nice and would bend over backwards to please everyone. I thought I was a pretty good mother, had always been a great worker, an excellent secretary and tried hard never to make a mistake.

To be anything less would have been shameful!

Part Two of *Homecoming* is about reclaiming the wounded inner child. Bradshaw has divided childhood/adolescence into four developmental stages based on Erik Erikson's map of psychosocial development. The aim is to revisit these stages, to grieve whatever needs were unmet, and to reclaim what we missed out on.

I could not believe how this book was EXACTLY what I needed. He had written it ten years earlier, but it was like he had written it for me! It was making sense of my breakdown. I hadn't gone crazy: I had just become aware that I was living a lie. I was living what I thought was expected of me, rather than living like the true me who was still buried deep.

I felt a sense of excitement. I thought I had fallen apart and I needed to pull myself together – instead, I realised that I needed to fall apart to find myself. **In other words, I needed to lose myself to find myself.**

In other words, I needed to lose myself to find myself.

Of course, as I soon found out, it wasn't going to be easy. In fact, it would be exhausting! I was about to become grief-stricken, sad, amazed, happy, angry, amused, bemused, fascinated and dumbfounded – just to name a few.

Bradshaw suggests that you support your child self by being the adult. I refer to these conversations with myself later on. I would be **Adult Heather (AH)** talking to **Young Heather (YH)**.

My task was to write down the facts – as many as I could remember – during each developmental stage, complete the questionnaire in the book, practise the meditation pertaining to each stage and write with my non-dominant hand as my child self.

This was the start of my automatic writing: a tool that led to so many discoveries and brought up many memories which had been long forgotten. Automatic writing is pure magic – it opened a whole new world for me!

My support team was growing. I now had Jannelle, John Bradshaw and his book, and my adult self.

It was also important for me to understand that going into the past to look at old wounds didn't mean I forever wallowed in them, staying a permanent victim, but that I needed to truly grieve any gaps in my developmental stages before I could heal.

I think this is where we see people get stuck: they play the part of the victim forever, and they are bitter and sad. I didn't want to be that – I wanted to be happy!

Bradshaw also stresses that our parents weren't bad, it's just that so many people are like wounded three-year-olds walking around in adult bodies. The wounds may be extreme or mild.

•●•

I thought about my original family. I am a middle child, and I have an older sister Ros, and younger sister, Sue.

What about my parents?

My dad was the fun one! He would often bring us a bag of lollies on a Friday night, and he played board games with us. I remember him helping us to clean our rooms and I also remember some wrestling matches. One of my strongest memories is him stroking my head when they were trying to get us to have an afternoon nap. I loved that! I liked following him around. He was sociable and well liked in the community.

We had a family outing every second Sunday – after church, of course. We would go on a picnic, to the beach or on a bushwalk. And sometimes we would go to Luna Park! We were very fortunate.

Like most housewives of the 1950s and 1960s, Mum was in the kitchen most of the time. She always seemed to be busy, but there was something else I noticed. She often seemed 'far away'. She had the weight of the world on her shoulders and there was no time for fun.

She looked after us well, always had us organised for school, took us into town every school holidays – but only after she had taken us to the dentist! We often had neighbourhood kids at our house and she provided for all.

Our Christmases were amazing! I loved the lead up to Christmas – the carols, decorating the tree, wrapping presents – and the fact that it was school holidays. On Christmas morning we would be up at dawn. I was enthralled by the magic of it. Santa had been and had left what seemed like a mountain of presents. It was the best day of the year!

And Easter was the second-best day. I always heard the neighbours going to midnight Mass – then I would lie awake for a while and wonder if the Easter bunny had been. In the morning we would head to the loungeroom for the big Easter egg hunt! Our initials were carefully taped onto Easter eggs. I can remember the excitement of finding an egg, only to be disappointed if it wasn't my initial!

We really were the epitome of a good, middle-class family, growing up in Australia in the 1960s. We had a television, phone and a car – more than many had. We had annual holidays to Flynn's Beach at Port Macquarie and to the Blue Mountains.

So, remembering this, why on earth would I have any unmet needs? I've just painted the picture of an idyllic childhood with caring parents. While there were sometimes fights between us siblings, our parents never fought with each other – we never heard raised voices – there was no alcoholic parent, like John Bradshaw had, and there was a regular income. We sometimes received a smack for being naughty, but all in all we were a very stable, secure family.

When I thought about this, I wondered if I was just being self-indulgent. Did I really need to do this therapy? Maybe I just needed to 'get on with it.' Then again, I had spent the last few months in a terrible state and I had felt something wasn't right. I had been in The Pit of Depression all my life, so it wasn't wise to brush it aside – I needed to do it to find the missing pieces.

John Bradshaw discusses 'rationalising' in his book. He talks about the stages of grief, and this is one of them. I was wondering if I was fussing over nothing – becoming too precious – but I knew there was something wrong.

I understood what he was saying, but in some ways, I felt self-centred. I also felt guilty. Could I really do this where I may be blaming my parents? They had done the best they could do.

Jannelle explained to me that it wasn't about blame, it was about finding the parts of yourself that had been lost or had not been able to develop. It was important to just look at it through the eyes of your child self to move through the process. I needed to let the guilt go and give myself permission to express any grief, rage, anger or sadness that came along.

So finally, I said to myself, 'Okay I will stop rationalising. I will start with the first stage.'

• ● •

I started at the beginning of my life. The first developmental stage is birth to nine months. My job was to gather the facts of this time period, and I was also to gather all the facts I knew about my parents. These would be read aloud to Jannelle at my next visit.

During those two weeks, I spoke to Mum. I told her I was wanting to get some old photos sorted. As I talked about the photos, I asked her more. I would say I remembered our first house being dark and she would fill me in on more details. I already knew some of the story, but it was a good way to get more information.

Mum never thought anything of it. She was pleased I was doing a photo project — it was certainly better than talking about how depressed I was!

What I was starting was a project on myself — a study of me! My workspace was my bedroom: my bed to be exact. I liked my room, even though I didn't really like the house I was in. We had bought the house because it ticked the boxes we needed, not because we fell in love with it.

We had moved to Coffs Harbour a couple of years earlier. It had been my dream to get out of the city and back to a country area, and here we were, living the dream. But at that time my dream had become a nightmare.

I spent most of my time in my bedroom when I wasn't doing all my usual mothering jobs. It was still school holidays, so the kids got up late. If they weren't spending time with friends or going somewhere, they liked to spend time downstairs watching TV or playing some of the early computer games. They loved being at home and could entertain themselves. That left me plenty of time to spend on The Study of Myself!

Here I was at the very beginning of my journey back in time. I had no idea what I would discover!

•●•

MY LEARNINGS

- I realised the journey wasn't going to be easy – but when it's a matter of life and death, do the work, even if it's difficult.

- I also learnt that rationalising is a defence mechanism – I had to get past that and allow myself to go deeply into my childhood stages in order to reclaim those lost parts of myself.

- And finally, this Study of Myself was to be the most important study I was ever to do!

FOR THE READER

- 'Getting on with it' or rationalising is a form of denial.

- Having therapy is not self-indulgence, it is the best thing you can do for yourself.

- Do not fall into the victim trap – you deserve to grieve – but enjoy the beginning of a new you!

- Letting yourself fall apart is the bravest thing you can ever do.

Chapter Three

Finding Kindness And Love

'The wound is the place where the light enters you.'

— **Rumi**

'The best way out is always through.'

— **Robert Frost**

By the time I was due to see Jannelle again, I had gathered the facts of my first year. I felt a mixture of excitement and dread as I drove to the appointment. Here I was at the entry to a long, dark tunnel. The only way out was through and going through some parts would be tough. But I had no choice: if I stayed staring at the entry to the tunnel, my mind and my life would not improve. I was a mess physically and mentally and getting through each day in my present state was unbearable.

There was simply no choice. I sat down in Jannelle's office, opened my exercise book in which I had carefully written down as many facts as I could, and started to read aloud. I was entering the tunnel.

First, I read out details of my parents which I had written in a matter-of-fact way. It was only later that I thought about how their early lives had shaped them, and how tough it must have been to be involved in war – or had parents who had served in the war.

I started with Mum. She was born in 1922 in Gosford. Her parents had an orchard and dairy farm and her father had fought with the AIF in France during WWI. Mum had one older brother. When she was three years old her mother died from colitis, so Mum and her brother were sent to live with their grandparents who were very strict.

When she was six, her father remarried, and they returned to live with their father and his new wife. Her father and stepmother went on to have three boys and she was required to help with them. She told me she had suffered at school – the teachers were harsh, and she also found her brothers a torment.

However, she did well at school, but when WWII broke out, she wanted to help the army effort, but her father wouldn't allow it. She went on to obtain her leaving certificate and moved to Sydney to attend business college. She was thrilled to get away from the farm! She found work as a switchboard operator and was also a volunteer air raid warden.

After the war there was more tragedy in the family – her stepbrother was killed in a motorbike accident and her stepmother died, so she returned home to look after her dad, who soon married for a third time.

She also told me she was jilted by a fiancé, which devastated her.

(We later found out that she became pregnant to this fiancé. Unbeknown to her, the fiancé was already married with a child. She only told us about our half-sister Liz when she was in her 80s – a secret she kept to herself all those years.)

A couple of years later she met my father. She said it was a blind date, that she had been going to travel the world but instead she fell in love.

(Again, Mum told me in later years this story was not correct. She had suffered severe depression after she had Liz and was seeing a doctor at Gladesville hospital. The hospital had support groups for people suffering from depression and it was here that she met Dad, who was also being treated for depression.)

Dad was born in 1923 at Kenthurst, near Sydney. His mother had emigrated from rural Suffolk in England with her parents and younger siblings when she was 13, and his father had been a trooper and spent time in the Signal Corp with the Australian Light Horse in Palestine during WWI. He was 'very good with horses' according to his enlistment papers. After the war, Dad's father purchased a 'soldier's plot' of land at Kenthurst, and it was here that he grew up.

Dad was the eldest boy – his brother Ray was born six years later. He entered the war at age 18 and was stationed in Darwin. He was serving as an anti-aircraft gunner, guarding the airfield, when the town, harbour and airfield were bombed by the Japanese in February 1942.

After the war he returned to live with his family, who were now living in the city, and he worked for the T & G Mutual Life Insurance Society.

He married a family friend in the late 1940s – it was a marriage doomed from the start. The woman he married had talked herself into it: she knew she was attracted to women, but it was considered so wrong in those days. Finally, they realised it wouldn't work and he had to go through the trauma of having the divorce printed in the paper!

The effects of the war and the shame of divorce 'nearly finished him' according to his aunty and therefore he was being treated for depression, which of course led to meeting Mum, as mentioned previously.

They married in 1953 and had my sister Ros the following year. Dad was studying accountancy at night and working full time. He also did tax returns, so was very busy.

He was successful at work, popular – and according to Mum – the perfect husband and father. They had an idyllic marriage.

And for the time being, that finished up my short summary of both of my parents. I had read it aloud to Jannelle and so far, there hadn't been any time she had stopped me. So far, so good – now it was on to me!

I had written down all the facts I had gathered about my first nine months and proceeded to read them aloud.

I was born in 1956. I arrived in the world almost two years after my sister Ros, and I would end up being the middle child, with younger sister Sue arriving in 1959.

Mum had always rolled her eyes when she talked about my baby year. She said I was a small baby and skinny, I was on 'three-hourly feeds' and it was difficult! She also told me she didn't really have any breastmilk and I was bottle-fed from birth. I was an exhausting baby – I slept all day and was awake all night.

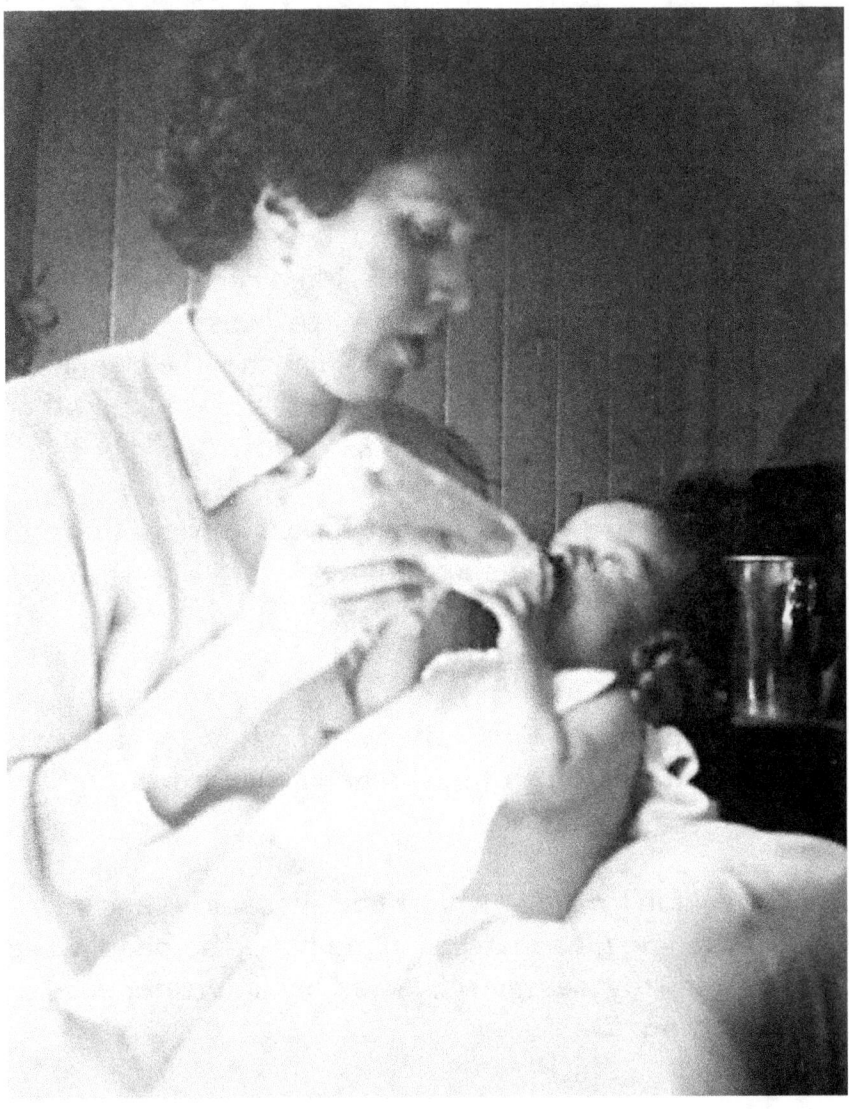

At the time I was born, each weekend my dad was helping the builders renovate the house and Mum was providing meals for them all. As well as having me, she also had a toddler – and like a good 1950s wife, she was trying to keep up with the housework.

She told me she was very resentful of all she had to do, but she kept quiet. On top of that, I was not gaining weight and the clinic sister was very concerned. I was a 'failure to thrive' baby. At each feed time I was also sat on the potty because she was obsessed with having me toilet-trained as soon as possible.

When I was just a few months old, Mum had a breakdown. She said she had been suffering since I was born and she collapsed one day while she was holding me. The neighbour took me in. Her name was Jessie, and she was a mother to five children. She was a very kind lady...

I read those words out and felt an ache in my throat. I started to cry. Jannelle stopped me.

'Tell me, what are you feeling?'

I sobbed, 'She was kind! She was excited to have me! She was interested in me! I wasn't an afterthought! I felt safe!'

Wow! I couldn't believe what I had just said – and I was crying! I had no idea that was in me buried so deeply. The words 'kind lady' set me off. It was my first experience of true nurturing.

Jannelle replied, 'So, the tears aren't because you were taken away, it was because she cared about you?'

'Yes!' I said. 'I wasn't a nuisance to her – she enjoyed having me! I wasn't scared!'

Jessie consulted with the doctor about changing my formula and tried different combinations. Mum told me they settled on Carnation Milk and Pentavite and 'I never looked back.' I was much more content when I finally returned from my time there. I had gained weight and was smiling!

Five years after my therapy had finished, I found out the truth about why I was placed in Jessie's care. During my daily meditation, I'd had a vision of myself as a baby and I was being thrown. I felt shocked and cheated – cheated out of babyhood – and I was angry.

Next time I saw Mum, I asked her. I had to be careful as I didn't want to lay blame. I approached it carefully, talking about my own postnatal struggles. Mum finally told me the truth. She had severe postnatal depression and had struggled from the day I was born. I had indeed been thrown. I was eventually taken from her as it was feared she would kill me.

The neighbour had heard the commotion one day when it all got too much. In fact, Jessie probably saved my life – and that's why I cried when I mentioned her and why I repeated that I felt safe. She was the first kind lady in my life, and no doubt she is the reason I'm here today. She saved Mum too, for who knows what would have happened if I had been killed.

I have never blamed Mum. Postnatal depression is a terrible thing, and back then there was no support. This wonderful neighbour took both Ros and I in while Mum got much needed rest and help.

Mum had previously been treated for depression after the 'shame' of finding herself pregnant and being rejected by her former fiancé. Then she kept the 'terrible secret' to herself. No wonder she suffered again. It was just sad for me that I was in the firing line.

And that ended all I knew of my first nine months. I sat still, taking in what had just happened. I felt a mixture of sadness, appreciation and disbelief as I could not believe that had been sitting inside of me my whole life! I had been searching for that kindness and caring and, at the time of my birth, my poor mother was in no state to be able to give me that.

It explained the disconnect I had always felt with Mum – the lack of emotional connection.

Jannelle suggested that I go through the infant meditation with her. Then in the future I could do the others at home.

Little did I know it, but this first meditation was to be THE most powerful experience I had ever had! And to this day – it still is!

In John Bradshaw's book, there is a general meditation which guides you to relax, then there is another part for each particular stage.

First, we went through relaxation and following the breath in and out. I had experienced guided meditations before, so much of this was familiar. I was transported to my baby self and guided to look around to see who was with me.

I had a vision of myself lying in the cot, and I was staring at the ceiling, waiting, just waiting to see a face… but no one came. I was alone.

I called out, 'But there is no one! My parents aren't here! I'm alone!' I had become my baby self, and I could feel what I went through. I was helpless, I felt such despair and sadness – my baby self had felt that and held it inside all those years… but in that very moment, I saw something else!

I was still fully as my baby self and now there was a brilliant white light in front of me – and I felt it throughout my entire body. I have never felt so loved, so nurtured, so cared for. At that moment, in every fibre of my being, I felt truly alive, truly loved. I was at peace. As I type this now – over 20 years later – I have tears in my eyes.

The love felt warm, pure, healing and uplifting – and ever so powerful. It was otherworldly, but also familiar. I'm not religious in the traditional sense, but it felt like something greater than myself, but also part of myself. It was such a gift and honour to feel it. Yes, honour; I still feel so honoured that I was able to experience that moment.

I sat with that feeling for some time. Then, when the meditation was finished, I described it to Jannelle. We talked about it.

I asked, 'So I haven't gone crazy?' Jannelle responded, 'Not at all! It will help to fill that emptiness inside of you.'

I left our session with such a sense of lightness…. and a knowing. It seemed that there was much more to this world we lived in. Unexplainable things were happening. Yet deep within me, somewhere, I already knew – I had just forgotten that I knew!

In those next couple of weeks I had an urge to run up to people and shake them - I wanted them to feel what I had felt. Of course, they would have thought I was crazy, but I wanted everyone to experience it. I thought it would help all the sad souls out there. This isn't how things work though. And that wasn't my job. My job was to continue with the Study of Myself.

With the kids returned to school, I now had more time to myself. I had deferred my studies indefinitely; at that point in time, the degree course seemed very trivial. Where it was once so important, now all that mattered was the exploration of myself!

My next task was to start writing. I wrote to the child, Young Heather, from my adult self. It felt like a weird thing to do. Would this really help? Well, I started like this, as outlined in the book, *Homecoming*, but it led to so much more!

Dear Young Heather,

I'm so honoured to be looking after you. We are going to have fun! You are very special.

Love,

Adult Heather

Dear Adult Heather,

I'm excited you found me. I'm so lonely. No one wants to be with me. No one is laughing. Please keep me company.

Love,

Young Heather

This writing back and forth was to become a great way for me to get in touch with myself – it led to even more writing. This was to be a major factor in my healing. I was determined to do all I could to heal myself, so I became as determined in this course as I had been in my university course. For me, this was life and death: if I didn't get through it, I would never truly live. I would just exist.

In my daily life there had been some changes. I dropped out of volunteer work at the school. I had always volunteered, but now was the time to let others take over. I was in no state to do it.

The one thing I kept going was my new Adventure Girls group. The group met once or twice a month for an activity.

The Adventure Girls outings were a pleasure. It was something for me, even though some days I had to force myself out. I was always so glad I did! I could at least feel normal for a day. I was also making new friends and we laughed together through our various adventures!

I also started horse-riding each week. I would attend a 'ladies morning' at our local trail riding centre. These days were so healing, and while I was exhausted most of the time, I always had energy for riding!

•●•

In one of my early sessions with Jannelle, she asked me how I viewed myself. I said I felt I was very conservative – we were a conservative family. She disagreed – she thought I was far from conservative. She said, 'There aren't that many people who would just start up a group like Adventure Girls. That's not what a conservative person would do!'

That statement empowered me. I hadn't thought of it like that. It was exciting to think that I may be a little offbeat! I often smiled at that thought – or more the thought that Mum would be horrified if people saw me as something other than conservative!

So much had come out from my first year on earth. I hadn't had the best of starts. Already there had been so much trauma — trauma that I never knew existed until I undertook this intensive study. It explained so much. The fear had been there from day one of my life.

MY LEARNINGS

🦋 The Study of the Self is the most important thing we can do. Self-absorption is needed to do this – and that's okay.

🦋 Gathering the facts about my life and reading them out loud proved to be way more powerful than I thought. It allowed buried feelings to arise, such as the feelings surrounding the kind lady next door.

🦋 The discovery of the white light through the guided meditation has had a huge impact on my life. We are not alone – and true love is always with us.

FOR THE READER

🦋 Reading aloud to someone about your life is a powerful experience. If you need to, seek out a professional.

🦋 When you are in a safe space, with someone who understands, you can fully explore yourself. Do not be afraid when unexpected feelings arise. Let them out!

🦋 I hope you are also able to experience the sense of love and peace I felt through the appearance of the white light. It may appear to you as something different. It changed everything.

Chapter Four

Meeting The Child Within

'What lies behind us and what lies before us are tiny matters compared to what lies within us.'

— **Ralph Waldo Emerson**

'They tell me there are many gods, for god is in each of us.'

— **Dr. Brian Weiss**

The next two weeks were spent gathering information about my toddler years. I found myself looking forward to the next session. After the amazing moment with the first meditation, I felt more confident. For the first time in my life, I felt like someone was on my team!

I took my notes out about the toddler years and started to read aloud to Jannelle.

Mum recovered from her breakdown/depression, and I went home from the neighbours stronger and happier. As I started to move more, Ros and I played all day together. Here is a photo of Mum holding me and we are both smiling – I think a first in my short life!

Nanna (Dad's mother) spent time with us, and we also visited my grandpa and grandma. I remember that our grandma would take us on outings and we really enjoyed our time with her.

Mum said I didn't really have tantrums and apparently after my newborn stage, I was 'easy.' I apparently never wet the bed and I was out of nappies early. I think I was shamed for not behaving correctly.

I felt that Mum was still busy – I was a bit of a nuisance. And I don't think touching or cuddling were really allowed… I also don't think I was allowed to be angry or sad, like it was an unwritten rule….

Jannelle asked me about being an easy child. This time there had been no tears, but a feeling of resignation… Even at that young age I was trying to be as little trouble as possible. As we talked, I felt a sadness that I hadn't truly bonded with Mum. She seemed far away. I felt like I was a burden.

I thought about my relationship with my own children while driving home from the session.

As a parent myself, I also struggled with postnatal depression for a short while – not in a severe way – but I understand what a terrible time it can be. Even so, I felt such joy in watching my kids grow and there were many cuddles every day. I had already noticed that their upbringing was very different to mine.

They were breastfed on demand, woke in the night, wet the bed and weren't toilet-trained until the average age, which I think is two to three years.

> I finally worked out what was missing. It had been niggling at me: it was JOY!

I finally worked out what was missing. It had been niggling at me: it was JOY!

I didn't feel any joy from Mum! She did all the correct things – but she didn't really see me. I wasn't seen! She went through the motions, but there seemed to be a wall between us.

My sadness started to turn to anger. I could feel it bubbling up. This was a good thing – it needed to come out.

When I arrived home from our session, I fell on the bed, and slept for several hours. This was to become a common theme – sleeping was as much a part of the healing process as everything else. Many days were spent working on myself, followed by sleeping in the afternoon. I normally drove down the hill to get my kids from the school bus, but many days I slept through.

They would arrive at the door and call out, 'Mum, we're home! You're asleep!' I would wake up feeling so guilty. How could I sleep all afternoon?

Many years later, my son Matt said to me, 'Mum, remember when you were on the bed all the time?' It was something that had stuck in his memory. Their mother who had always been so on the ball, had seemingly lost it! And I guess I had – I had to lose myself to find myself.

I told some people I had chronic fatigue – it was the easiest thing to say. However, I did tell some friends I had depression. Several friends dropped away... they would ring to tell me their troubles and I had always been a good listener. Now I just couldn't listen so I would tell them I wasn't in a good place and had depression. Several times those words were met with silence, then something like this... 'Oh, that's no good. I hope you feel better soon.'

The phone stopped ringing so often – those people just dropped away. When I couldn't fulfil their needs, they sought attention elsewhere. **As my false self dropped away, my false friends did also.**

It's an interesting process when you aren't behaving as you normally do. There were people who had previously taken up hours of my time who never rang again, never inquired as to how I was. I had kept my breakdown a secret from my sisters and pretended to Mum that I had forgotten about it.

But there was one friend who was there for me. I had met her while living in Wauchope on the mid north coast of NSW. Her name is also Janelle. I would receive her letters and cry as there was empathy and understanding. She actually saw me! I will be forever grateful to her.

I learnt that very few people saw me. This wasn't a fault of theirs — it was how I had behaved and adapted myself. I attracted the sort of people who were self-absorbed. In changing my awareness, these people were no longer attracted. They no doubt disappeared to seek out others who would fulfill their needs.

The following day I wrote to my child self. The anger had been building inside me.

I was amazed at how powerful these letter-writing sessions were! They really did make a difference! At first, I had thought of this as very self-absorbed, but this self-absorption is what is needed in order to properly delve into who we are!

The writing to my younger self continued. She was a very demanding toddler now that she felt safe. And often angry. The anger flowed out to the family, mainly to my husband Doug.

I made more demands on him. Why wasn't he spending more time with the family? Why didn't he want to go anywhere? Why was he often cranky and subdued? Why did he not want to spend time with me?

The angry, demanding toddler continued to cause chaos – although it wasn't really chaos. As I learnt, when we embrace some of these behaviours that were forbidden when we were young, like anger, the pendulum can swing too far into that behaviour before it comes back to middle ground.

I had done some study on family dynamics and knew how each family member can take on a role. We tend to get labelled as, for instance, the angry one, the funny one, the quiet one, the peacemaker etc.

My older sister, Ros, was allowed to express anger and tears, while I was the peacemaker and the funny one and Sue was the quiet one. I wasn't allowed to cry or shed tears, or I was shamed, even if it was in a joking way. The roles tend to fall into place naturally. One thing that the three of us learnt early on was not to expect affection. There was no cuddling, hugging, kissing – it was a foreign thing.

I spent several weeks with my toddler self. We wrote back and forth. I was finding the writing such a powerful way to communicate and to help bring out the buried feelings.

This is when I started to venture off the plan in the book *Homecoming* and into my own style of communication. While I started writing with my non-dominant hand, I quickly moved to my writing hand. The words flowed just as easily.

During the back-and-forth chat, we got to know each other. I found out she was so worried about being rejected. She wanted friends who wouldn't reject her. She wanted laughter and fun. She was happy I was noticing her.

I did the toddler meditation at home and asked Young Heather how it was. She replied, 'I was noticed. You value me!' I replied, 'Of course I do!'

Here is part of one of the many conversations I had:

> **AH: I can look after you now. And you know that your family, your mum and friends love you. And you felt the white light – that was true love... Why are you crying?**
>
> YH: Because the light is trying so hard to help me. It was with me all the time as a baby when no one else was. It's always with me. It wants me to remember why I'm here. I feel like I'm on the verge of something. That love is overwhelming. I feel stronger. I'm not as scared...

Tears flowed. She'd known all along it was with her... My child self knew! I felt so full, so grateful. I could feel physical changes in my body as I held onto the feeling of love. I had to name it: it was my true friend.

I called it God – I couldn't think of anything else. It certainly wasn't the God that had been taught to me at Sunday School. The feeling of love wasn't just within me, it was around me – connected to everything. It was a universal love. God became like a life coach, best friend and parent all wrapped up together.

I started writing to my new best friend. I took another A4 journal book and called it my God book. This was my first writing:

God, why does this touch me so deeply? I can't stop crying about it.

Because you've remembered – it's a powerful feeling.

Well, if I've remembered why do I still have this fear? Why do I need to finish this childhood process?

Because there's unresolved grief – you need to deal with it step by step.

Why can't everyone feel the love I felt?

Not everyone's ready. You've been looking for it for a long time. You've decided to stop and listen. Not many people do.

What do I do now? I want to share it with someone, but my family thinks I'm mad! I'm not cleaning the house; I'm not doing anything else – I just want to write – I can hardly stop! I think I'm obsessed!

Why should you stop? Remember, you have nothing to fear. This is important for you to understand Heather. NOTHING TO FEAR. I am with you all the time. Come and hang on to me. I'm pleased you've 'seen the light' (ha ha)! You're ready for some wonderful things that will give you and others absolute joy. I am with you always – everywhere – all ways. I'm the love you longed for – I know your greatness. I want you to know it. You're ready – finally in this life you are ready! You've remembered me. Do what your soul wants. LISTEN to yourself. LISTEN. Say goodbye to

fear. My love for you is unending, you need no other love. So off you go now and find joy!

I stared at the page and the words on it. I felt like I was in a movie, a fairy tale movie where I had found my fairy godmother!

I kept staring at the words. 'Look what I just wrote!' I thought. Where on earth had this come from? Why was it happening now? They were such nice words, powerful words, loving words. In this life, I had remembered…

'Is life about remembering?' I thought. 'Is that the meaning of life? Are we here to remember that we carry that love around - that we really do have a guardian angel? Or is it a built-in part of us that somehow I managed to access?' I really didn't know, but it didn't matter. I was just so happy to find it.

I moved on from the toddler stage, feeling more empowered. I wasn't so scared of changes in my life. I was getting better each day, although the tears weren't far away, even on the good days - the tear tap would never quite turn off. Sometimes I was just exhausted from the crying, but I knew that it would be the norm as I crawled through the tunnel of memories.

But now I had love to help me – unconditional love. It had been with me all along.

• ● •

MY LEARNINGS

- Writing to the child self is like magic. It played a major part in understanding myself and learning who I really was.

- As 'friends' dropped away, I wasn't bothered, but I did learn how I had attracted such needy people, because I was so desperate to 'fit in.'

- My child self continued to amaze me! I was really starting to discover the real me!

FOR THE READER

- The changes that come from doing this may create chaos at home – but just ride it out and understand that things will level out eventually!

- If you find friends dropping away, don't worry! Trust the process. In no time you will find new friends who fit the new you!

- Doing this type of therapy will create exhaustion. Needing to sleep all afternoon is nothing to worry about. It's part of the healing process!

- My wish is for you to find that unconditional love. Once you have found it, you will feel so empowered. I called it God – you can call it anything you like!

Chapter Five

Darkness In The Sun

'No power so effectually robs the mind of all its powers of acting and reasoning as fear.'

— **Edmund Burke**

The 1950s and 1960s were years of great prosperity in Australia. They were also what I refer to as the 'halcyon days' of our family unit.

My younger sister, Sue, was born in 1959 and we moved to a bigger and better house in Harrison Avenue, Eastwood – a suburb of Sydney. I loved this house! It was on the top of a hill and there were plenty of other kids to play with. This is when I met my best childhood friend, Kath, who lived across the road. We spent many an hour playing in the street, climbing the tree on the footpath and playing in various backyards.

Most mothers in that time were homemakers. Their life revolved around daily chores, but they had time to chat to each other. There was a real community atmosphere that is not felt so much these days. In the mornings, the men would leave the house to walk to the train station – you would see them going each morning – and we would laugh that, Paul, the boy from next door, would be seen running past our house with his piece of toast in his mouth and an apple. We regularly played with his sister Margie who we all adored. She was several years older than Ros and was like a big sister.

When Ros and Kath started school, I was alone all day. Mum was busy with Sue, and I can remember how bored I would get. I seemed to wander aimlessly around the house. In those days you didn't jump in the car and drive to a shopping centre or a fast-food outlet. Three- and four-year-olds didn't go to preschool. They were reserved for working parents.

I talked to my child self about those times. In fact, I had started to have long written conversations. She was restless and bored, she wanted to know about the world, so I played the 'What If' game with her. This is a game I played often with my child self. It gave me an idea of her truest thoughts and what she could have been in a perfect world. In other words, it helped me to find the truest essence of myself.

> **AH: Let's play a game – what if I was your best friend to laugh with – what would we do?**
>
> YH: Well, we would make my room really pretty. It would have fairies and princesses, butterflies and pinkish colours. We would stick stars on. I like stars. I'd have a net over my bed – I wouldn't be scared at night. I'd have chairs and a place to sit and read. There would be books about fairies.

AH: So, you would have a little library?

YH: Yes, the other kids could use it if they were neat. And when we finish reading, we would eat and laugh.

AH: Once we were done, then what?

YH: Then we would ride our horses. Mine is so beautiful and he can fly – he has wings!

AH: He's magic!

YH: Yes – he looks after me and keeps me safe!

AH: Where are we going to?

YH: We are flying through the clouds to a magic kingdom! It's where the kind ladies live! They have beautiful dresses and everyone smiles. The ladies are so kind and gentle – they teach us magic spells – good spells! There are spells to help all the animals! They have a beautiful library and we can go there and read! We can eat ice cream there and cakes! They are funny too! And they are always interesting.

AH: Wow! That sounds great! But… you're crying…

YH: Because I want to live with the kind ladies! It's such fun and I'm not scared. And our horses live with us. That's where I want to live forever!

• ● •

Again, I rocked back and forth, sitting on the bed, sobbing. I had entered the Kingdom of the Kind Ladies and it felt just right. Every moment was exciting, and our horses were just part of the family! I never wanted to leave!

I needed to ponder the emotion that came with this. **I was slowly learning who my child self was – or rather – who my TRUE self was.**

And the longing. Was I longing for another world? Another type of life? This was coming from my four-year-old self.

> I was slowly learning who my child self was – or rather – who my TRUE self was.

I tried to pull apart the longing, the yearning... what did I feel when I was there? I felt safe, I felt included, my mind was occupied, and I lived with the horses... the horses...

I continued these written conversations. Some were fairly routine, but others, like the story above, stayed with me. The writing helped me to feel stronger, like I was peeling away the layers – digging away to find myself within.

During a session, I told Janelle that in this period, our home life was good. I used to ask dozens of questions. I thought my parents were the smartest people in the world: they seemed to know all the answers!

Mum and Dad went to balls with the Masonic Lodge. I loved seeing Mum dressed up – she looked like the Queen! We had our Nanna look after us – Dad's mother. Our grandfather (Mum's father) died in 1960. Our grandma (his third wife) apparently wanted to keep seeing us, but Mum didn't allow it. That made me sad…

Jannelle stopped me and we discussed my grandma. Even though Mum didn't like her, she was so kind! She sent books and cards, and she was the only person who called me 'darling.' I liked that. It made me feel special. She was really interested in me… and then I never saw her again…

I didn't know why Mum wouldn't let her see us at the time. We were her grandchildren, even if not blood related. When Mum told me that she begged to see us after she was widowed, I just couldn't understand why she wouldn't show some compassion towards her. Now I understand that her stepmother knew of the secret of the pregnancy before marriage – and the stress of someone knowing was just too much for her.

I liked our Nanna visiting. She'd bounce us on her knee, and she'd let us crawl all over her. She would always show us three rings she wore and tell us which ring was ours when she died. The diamond ring was for Ros, the emerald for me and the ruby for Sue. It fascinated me. There was something about her picking out which ring she had left for us that was very special…

She died in the early 70s, but no rings were forthcoming. Mum said Nanna's sisters took them – and we were furious! In later years, Mum told us she had made up that story. She had in fact sold them as she needed the money... I couldn't believe she would do that. I felt so angry that my special ring from Nanna was gone – it was a violation of the link Nanna had with her grandchildren. The rings weren't valuable, they were only of emotional value. As an adult, I understand Mum's desperation for money, but I so wish she had consulted with us.

•●•

I entered the school system before I was five and I can remember being both excited and scared. Kath would take me each morning to put my playlunch in the box, which the teacher then handed out, and she helped me find a spot for my bag.

I can still remember the smell of the corridor – it smelt like my children's school bags when an uneaten sandwich came home! And I remember wetting my pants – not an unusual thing for a kindergarten child, but for me it was appalling! I just didn't normally wet my pants! This happened because the teacher wouldn't let me go to the toilet. I had queued up at lunch time to go, then the bell rang, so I thought I would be in trouble if I didn't immediately go to class. My bladder just couldn't hold it for the whole afternoon!

It sounds like such a small thing, and everyone would have a similar story, but for me, I was so ashamed. I had been conditioned at a young age that you do not wet your pants – and I had failed.

I did further writing on the pants-wetting episode. It was my first experience of shame in front of people in the outside world. My peers laughed at me, and so reinforced my early childhood experiences of feeling lesser. A seemingly small incident, I learnt, can have a compounding effect on your thought processes, especially when young.

The foundations were being laid for the road map in my brain – and the road labelled 'lesser' was becoming bigger and bigger.

I skipped a year of school – the transition year – when a new scheme came into the state schooling system. My parents were concerned but were assured I would manage. At the time I was excited, because now I was in class with my best friend Kath! When I look at that move through adult eyes, I was way too young to move up a year. Socially, I would always be a step behind.

The following year I had Mrs Lovell as a teacher. Everyone liked her, and I did too – until the incident.

I remember sitting in class listening to her talk and the girl at the desk behind me started tapping my shoulder trying to get my attention. I turned around to her and said 'What?' The next thing I knew, Mrs Lovell hauled me out of the chair and smacked me. I was so shocked, and the girl that started it was horrified! I was humiliated... but I didn't cry. I just wanted to melt into the floor. I hated that teacher from that day on...

How could she turn from normal to psycho in a split second? Again, I wrote more about this in my journal. It was the shame! I was so ashamed... I thought of myself as such a good little girl. I always tried to do the right thing, and I always had anxiety running through me at school.

A naughty boy may have brushed it off, an outspoken girl may have argued with the teacher, but for me I froze. It was nothing to do with the pain of the smacking, or the teacher's rough handling of me – it was to do with the shame. And so, the highway of shame was gradually becoming larger in my brain.

But 1964 was a sunny year as I had the best teacher! Her name was Mrs Mason and I remember her pleated skirts. Kath and I sat at the front of the class, and it was a very happy year; not only because of my nice teacher, but around the world, Beatlemania had spread. Ros and I had it as well!

Unless you were around at the time, it's hard to describe the effect Beatlemania had on the world. We were lucky to watch them on TV – in fact, we lived and breathed them. We collected any articles on them, and when they came to Australia in June of 1964, it was like a dream come true. I was only eight, but I wanted to go to their concert!

It really was like a happy virus. I was surprised our parents didn't really mind them and let us indulge in our obsession. We would sing along when their songs played on the radio, and the words to many songs have been embedded in my brain forever! Their presence brought an uplifting energy to the whole world. They were the messengers of this time, and they had a huge impact on the culture of the 60s.

It was suddenly cool to be young! I'm on the tail end of the Baby Boomer generation and we were so cool. This generation rebelled against the rules of the time. We were all heavily influenced by the Beatles, and no doubt many of us look back on that time as magical. They really have been the soundtrack of my life.

We had holidays to the beach and the mountains – we piled into our brand new 1964 EH Holden, Mum in the front with Dad at the wheel, and the three of us in the back. I can still remember the radio playing the latest Beatles songs while we drove to Port Macquarie. We were in the back seat singing *'I Feel Fine'* and *'Day Tripper'* and everything was sunny and fun. We would spend a week or two swimming fearlessly at Flynn's Beach – taking our blow-up surf mats out to the back row of the surf, getting sunburnt, eating pies, fish and chips and ice cream. It was the perfect summer holiday!

We also had outings every second weekend, and Mum regularly took us to Ryde Swimming Pool. I loved swimming – it was the one sport I was quite good at – and I loved our days there. Mum was so good! Our car was often loaded up with the neighbourhood kids as well – there were no such things as seatbelts then – and we would all swim until we were totally waterlogged!

The following year, however, became The Year of Mrs Davies.

Kath and I still sat right at the front, and we were fresh from the kindness of Mrs Mason. We were soon to learn that Mrs Davies didn't possess an ounce of kindness.

Some days she was just okay, other days she was crazy. This time though, every child was in the firing line. Kids were made to stand in the corner all day and one boy had to stand on his head. I was sick with fear. I would sit watching her as she wrote on the board. Despite my fear, my focus would go to the hairs on her legs – all curled up under her stockings! 'My, what hairy legs you have!' I would think to myself.

My weakness became maths due to the fearful environment. I had been fine with maths the year before, but one mistake led to a lifetime of maths struggles. One day we were working on multiplication. Mrs Davies would walk up and down the lines of desks and everyone was so very quiet. On this particular day, as she walked past me, she saw something.

I was hauled out of my chair and smacked repeatedly – it seemed to go on forever, like she had so much anger to release. Then she pushed me back into my seat and screamed, 'Your multiplication sign goes above the line, not on it!' The screams were from a madwoman. I sat there with my head down and the tears rolled. I was now so ashamed of not only being pulled out of my chair, but for appearing to be so stupid as to not know where the sign should be written.

This is as fresh in my memory as if it were yesterday. It's not to do with the physical belting, it's all to do with the emotional abuse.

This must have been the more severe day of punishment for me, but there were others. It was a very scary year at school.

I never mentioned these events at home. I was too ashamed, but I would tell Mum I was sick so I could stay home the next day. As we grew up and I talked about Mrs Davies, Mum said she did wonder why I wanted to be home that year but thought I must have had a bad year with childhood sickness. She said I would lie in bed quietly and stare at the ceiling. **I was suffering from shock. Yet Mum didn't see it. She just didn't see me!**

> I was suffering from shock. Yet Mum didn't see it. She just didn't see me!

I became sick during this part of the therapy, and I knew it was because of the Mrs Davies memories.

I had conversations with my young self quite often about how what I was experiencing in the present moment was related to childhood memories.

> **AH: What's wrong Young Heather? Why are you sick?**
>
> YH: I'm scared to get better – because I will have to face the outside world.
>
> **AH: I gather we are talking about Mrs Davies.**
>
> YH: Yes.
>
> **AH: Well, what happened was awful. You could only hide at home by being sick, couldn't you? You couldn't say you were scared; your Mum would have ridiculed you. And you certainly couldn't tell your Mum what happened. But your Mum fears the outside world too – and you picked up on that early.**
>
> YH: Other people are superior, we are taught. If I tell, they will yell or ignore me.
>
> **AH: Why do you think that?**
>
> YH: Mum doesn't want to know about me. I'm a bother. Mrs Davies thinks I'm an idiot. Everyone is more grown up. At home I can be safe. My bed feels good. Mum is nicer to me when I'm sick.
>
> **AH: So being sick has lots of rewards. Well, let's play the 'what if' game. What if school was**

friendly and exciting? What if your teachers were kind? What if your Mum hugged you and was interested in you? Would you fear anything?

YH: No. I'd be enthused. If I was scared, I could tell Mum and she would listen and hug me. I would be confident…

AH: Well, don't forget now you have me. And don't forget about God – there really is nothing to fear! We are your team! You're crying?

YH: I never had a team. I can feel you caring. I think I can do it. God is helping me. I've got lots to do. Now I can cope with Mrs Davies. You'll both watch over me.

AH: Of course we will!

I realised that the missing link was being too scared to ask for support from my parents. I was scared because I thought it was all my fault – I didn't need to be in trouble again. I knew that Mum wouldn't understand. In those days, parents tended to side with the teacher. The teacher was God in their eyes and the children were always wrong. But I was too scared to even test whether they would support me. It was easier just to pretend to be sick.

When my daughter Emma was in primary school, she had a teacher, Mrs J, who ridiculed her in front of me. I watched Emma hang her head in shame. The teacher had said to me 'Your daughter – where has she been? Why doesn't she know (whatever it was she was meant to know)?'

She was starting the new year with this teacher after having a year of kindergarten, and Mrs J had also taught my son Matt the year before. She had taken a dislike to me and to Matt because she just didn't understand him. She would say to me, 'I don't know where your boy is, but he's not with us!' I asked her to explain, knowing full well that Matt would never fit the box that she was trying to put him in.

She told me he was always staring out the window, but he seemed to know the answer when she asked him. I said, 'So he knows the answer, what is the problem?' She insisted that he needed to see the school counsellor, so I arranged an appointment. After the counsellor had seen him, she spoke to me and laughed! 'There's nothing wrong with him! He's fine. The problem is with the teacher who just doesn't understand him!'

In fact, when we asked Matt what he was thinking in class, he would say he was often looking at the screws and bolts in the building and wondering what they were for. He would also be thinking about the universe. One time at this age he asked us if the universe kept expanding outwards. This is what was in his head as he stared out the window!

So here I was again with this teacher challenging me and Emma. I was furious she could be so careless in talking about Emma in front of her, to create such shame. The next afternoon I made an appointment to see her. I met her alone and lost my temper.

All the bottled-up issues I had had with school came flowing out. At one point I clenched my fist and thought I would punch her! I was screaming! 'How dare you talk about her in front of her. You ask where she has been? Well, she has been right here at this school – if you have a problem with her learning, you had better talk to her teacher from last year! And I will say to you now – you have a set against our whole family!'

Mrs J looked terrified. She stammered, 'No – not at all!'

I spat words at her 'You couldn't understand Matt. You didn't like him because he didn't fit the mould. And when I took him to the counsellor, she laughed and said that he doesn't have a problem, the teacher does! You are so narrow, you lack understanding!'

She was still stammering, 'No, I think your son is exceptionally bright!'

'Well, what was the problem?' I screamed. She shook her head, seemingly in shock that gentle and kind Mrs Binns, who helped the children in her class with reading, had turned into a monster.

I kept screaming, 'Okay, we need to go right now to move Emma into another class – she is NOT going to be humiliated by you all year!'

'Oh, please Mrs Binns, I'm very happy to teach Emma!' she pleaded.

'Are you? Are you really? Well, this is what you must do. You now have made her so ashamed and fearful. You have an enormous amount of work to make it up to her. Do you think you can do that?'

'Oh, yes! I'm terribly sorry to have caused such upset,' she cried. Now tears were flowing from her – it gave me great satisfaction.

So, Emma continued in her class, and Mrs J showered her with compliments and stickers and special jobs. Emma went from being scared to just loving her. Mrs J treated me with a new respect. I had stood up for my children: I had given them what I had missed out on.

All my bottled-up anger for Mrs Davies and Mrs Lovell spewed out onto this teacher. I was fighting for myself as much as for my children. And I was doing what I wished my parents had done. I was sad – sad that I could never confide in them. But with my own children I had broken the cycle.

There is a balance to be had when dealing with teacher/child issues. I don't condone screaming at teachers. I did not handle it in the best way, but I know what is fair and right, and she was in the wrong in this instance.

Now, back to the story!

In 1966, Mum told us we were moving to Tamworth – a country town in NSW. I was frightened, but excited! I asked if I could learn to ride a horse and have a two-wheeler bike.

Dad had a big promotion. He was to be manager of the T & G insurance company for the whole north-western region of NSW which was a brand-new position. His photo was in the local paper – there was much excitement!

We went on our first ever plane ride to Tamworth to see our new house. We had brand new dresses for the occasion as plane travel was normally only for the wealthy! It was on this flight that we met Mrs Sear. Her husband also had a promotion, so we would be moving together. She was another kind lady! She hugged us, called us 'darlings' and shared our enthusiasm. Mum however was devastated. She didn't want to move and was happy in Eastwood.

We moved in the winter, so I finished 5th class at my new school in Tamworth. This primary school was so different. It was a much more relaxed place, and I made many friends in a short amount of time.

I loved our new house! It was newly built and was located at the start of the drive to the town lookout. We spent our time on our new bikes riding up and down the hill and exploring the mountain. We had amazing freedom! I loved the fact that the bush was so close, just over the road. There were so many adventures to be had. And in the afternoon, we could sit on our verandah and look out at the distant hills. Even then, I admired the beauty. I loved to sit and watch everything around me. I was so happy to be living in the country!

We were also given the horse-riding lessons as promised! The 'lesson' consisted of getting on a pony and helping the lady round up cows! She didn't teach us anything, and in fact the pony bolted for home the very first time I rode it. I cried, but hung on, and returned for more. I really loved it, despite the threat of being thrown off.

We spent our days at the local swimming pool in summer, and I improved on my swimming. I took to country life like a duck to water. I was so happy to leave city life behind and I wanted to stay there forever!

We still had to attend church and Sunday school, and Dad joined the local bowling club. He made lots of friends, but he was very busy. He travelled a lot, and we didn't see him as often...

In 1967, I was in my final year of primary school: 6th class. My teacher, Mr Rogers, was such a jolly man! I was starting to think I was pretty clever. I was getting great results in the new environment — in fact, I was in the top ten of the class! We went on excursions, and our weekends were full, either exploring or playing with other kids.

For the most part, my early childhood was happy, but at the same time I was unaware how much emotional damage the incidents described had affected my self-worth and learning ability. I had a child's naïve optimism and feeling of happiness.

However, in my 11th year, something happened which was to sweep away even my superficial happiness and leave me completely emotionally devastated...

MY LEARNINGS

- My emotion regarding the trip to the Kingdom of the Kind Ladies was overwhelming. I could feel the longing inside. What was I longing for? I wanted to be with adults who stimulated me and who were kind so I wouldn't be too scared to learn. And I wanted the animals, like the horses, to be part of the family. We could all be in a happy place together.

- I learnt that being sick allowed me to be safe. I could hide in my bed away from the scary world. My mother had not recognised I was in shock, but she thought I was sick enough to stay home.

- I learnt that I couldn't tell Mum if I was struggling with anything at school.

- I learnt that even as a child, I could see what was right or wrong – even when my parents didn't see it.

FOR THE READER

- If you feel a longing, like I did in regard to the Kingdom of the Kind Ladies, explore that feeling. Find out what it means for you.

- In the example of my grandmother and my Nanna's rings – it's important to explore the anger felt at the time. It's easy to rationalise it as an adult, but it represses the anger inside.

- Writing is healing – putting pen to paper lets you immerse yourself fully in a time long ago. Not only does it have a meditative effect, but it also gives you the space to allow memories to resurface.

- The 'What If' game is a great tool. I used it above in a conversation with my child self. It allows you to see what you would be like if the situation had been different.

Chapter Six

My World Crashes Down

'Fifty years after the death occurred, men and women still refer to the early death of a parent as the defining event of their lives.'

— Maxine Harris, PhD

Ever since we had moved to Tamworth, Dad had been under so much stress as the new job carried a massive workload. He became very sick and suffered heart trouble.

I remember him trying to create a garden. He wanted to plant rose bushes around the border of our block. I was out there helping him when Mrs Sear, the kind lady, arrived. She came over and hugged me. As she held my face in her hands, she said, 'You're better than two shining suns put together!' It was wonderful – I was noticed! I so rarely got positive comments. Those words have stayed with me for over 50 years!

Dad went back to work on and off and took up smoking again. I remember spending lots of time just sitting with him. I'd watch his hands shaking and feel so sorry for him. I wanted to fix it, but I didn't know how, so I just sat there on the lounge keeping him company.

By November, he had deteriorated and was spending his days in bed. We would go in to say goodbye before we left for school. On this particular day, November 10, he called us back in before we left. He said, 'I just wanted to see you all again.' He stared at us for a while – we were slightly puzzled, then off we went.

Around lunchtime that day, a friend of Mum's came to get me. When I saw her, I felt ill: I knew why before she said anything. She told me my dad was very sick and Mum wanted us all home. I knew that was wrong. I knew he was dead… but I didn't want to hear it. I struggled to walk to her car with shaky legs.

When we pulled up at our house there were dozens of cars there, and when we walked inside, we were surrounded by people. I sat in a lounge chair and poor Sue was given the arm of the chair – Ros was sitting over on the other lounge surrounded by people. Mum was across the other side of the room, crying. And then she said it – the words I didn't want to hear – even though I already knew:

'Girls, your dad died today.'

Then she cried some more… I sat still, the room felt dark, and I felt like I had been physically crushed. I wanted to die as well – how would we go on living now? I was 11 years old, and I wanted to die… My brain interrupted the shock for a second – it told me it was a joke. He wasn't really dead… no… they were wrong!

Then shock returned and every cell in my body felt like it was under attack. I couldn't breathe or move. And I couldn't cry. It was too much of a shock to cry. **In those seconds, I moved into a new version of myself.**

> I knew in those moments that the pain would be there forever.

The pain of the words entered every cell, into the depths of my heart. I knew in those moments that the pain would be there forever.

In my daze, I noticed Mum was saying something to one of the women, 'Oh, I think they are having a delayed reaction.' And the whole room was staring at us… I couldn't move. It hurt. And if I moved, I would be heading into a new life without my Dad, my beloved Dad, who was the glue of the family, who brought happiness in, who kept Mum happy…

How could I take one step into the future without him? My 11-year-old eyes could see nothing but bleakness… And I still sat and stared in disbelief. Ros was crying, but Sue and I sat still, no one came near us, but everyone was staring at us.

Why didn't the adults comfort us? They were hugging Mum, but no one was hugging us. It's strange the things you remember. It reinforced my lack of worthiness. I wasn't worthy of a hug, of a kind word. I could only be stared at like an animal at the zoo.

Still, I sat there and stared while millions of reactions were occurring inside.

I had the urge to see him – I wanted to see his body. Was he in the house still? I wanted to look.

Mum was saying that they went to the hospital that morning, but as they walked up the steps, he asked to sit down. And that's where he died… on the hospital steps. What a terrible shock for Mum. He was only 44.

No. Again my brain said it was a joke. We had just said goodbye as we left for school only four hours earlier! And then I remembered how he called us back to say goodbye again – how he stared at each one of us – taking us in. He knew it would be his last day on earth. No, this wasn't happening – it was a bad dream.

Then shock returned. The room looked grey. I wanted to run away – back to our life four hours earlier. How could I escape this new reality? It felt like forever that we had to endure the crowd of people in our loungeroom.

We were eventually herded into a bedroom, just the three of us, and left alone. We talked amongst ourselves, expressing disbelief, but I think mainly we sat there staring – trying to comprehend what we had been told. When we came out of the room people were still milling about, flowers were arriving, and Mum was still in pieces.

As evening came, the neighbour arrived with a casserole, and the four of us sat down to eat it. The four of us. Now we were a family of four – not five…

Dad's good friend was still there, I think trying to organise details. Mum suddenly burst out, 'Why is he here? Why doesn't he go away??' I tried to calm her. I said, 'He's only trying to help.' I was being the adult, and that's how I've felt ever since. I've spent the rest of my life trying to console my Mum.

The next day we were shipped off to friends for a few days. When I tried to talk about it to my friend, she looked frightened. I guess 11-year-olds don't really know what to say. I saw her discomfort, so I didn't mention it again... I had been taught well to consider others before myself, even though I desperately needed to talk about it.

By the time we arrived home after several days, the funeral had taken place and all Dad's clothes had gone. It was like he never existed. Why did he have to be swept away? Even the rooms were rearranged. Ros and I now had the main bedroom while Mum moved into the smaller one.

I remember I wanted to see his clothes, I wanted to talk about him.... But he was never discussed again. Never again...

Mum had said it was too sad for us to attend the funeral, and it was best to get rid of everything. It was even too sad to have a photo. It was also too sad to see his grave.

For the next 20 years, I didn't see a photo of Dad and I started to imagine if he was real. Did I really ever have a dad? Why couldn't we talk about him?

•●•

Imagine your family for a minute – you have your parents and your siblings. You are a child, going about your day. Then imagine you hear that one of your parents has died. One of two people who you rely on so heavily for everything – for love, security, guidance – a person who steers you through a world that is often bewildering and terrifying. They steer you through those parts and they show you how to make your way through the scary bits until you are old enough to manoeuvre through these parts yourself.

This person takes care of your physical needs, they provide the income to allow you to live in your home, to be clothed, to have food, to be looked after. They also provide for your emotional needs – even if they are not always there, they are the main provider of those needs – even if those needs aren't fully met.

This person also looks after the other parent. They help them with their insecurities, they give them love and they give them financial security.

So, you've just heard that this person is dead – they no longer exist. Your child's brain has difficulty processing it. You are scared – in fact, terrified – and you are completely devastated. Completely.

How does a child pick up the pieces? Well, one thing they desperately need is to talk about the deceased parent. In fact, they need to talk about their deceased parent for the rest of their lives. They need memories, they need to know what their parent was like. They want to know all about them. They need to know their history, what they liked, what they didn't like.

They need a physical reminder – maybe they need some clothing, their watch, even their comb! Something! And they need photos of their parent at different ages, so they can get a complete sense of what their parent was like.

This is only a small part of what a child needs. But sweeping them away, never to be mentioned again, is not only damaging beyond words – it is quite sick. I would also add that it is selfish.

For the parent left, while they may be consumed with grief, they must give their children support, they must consult with them on the grieving process.

• ● •

For us, Dad became a forbidden subject. It had shades of the Fawlty Towers refrain, 'Don't mention the war.'

My World Crashes Down

I had a few days off school, and when I went back it was obvious that the whole class had been informed. Everyone was so nice to me. I was so well supported, but no one actually mentioned it. We only had a few more weeks at primary school before we finished for the long summer break.

Home life in those weeks was grim. In the first week after he died, I kept playing a game in my head. I would say, 'This time last week he was still alive.' I just wanted to go back in time. The pain was unbearable — I just wanted to see him again. It was a feeling of suffocation. I wanted to wake up from this nightmare... but that wasn't to be.

Our neighbour from Eastwood, Kath's mother, came to stay for a week. It was very good of her. I still have a vivid memory of her leaving as I was watching from the window. Mum waved her goodbye, then turned around and burst into tears. I felt so sorry for her. I just wanted to fix it. Why did this have to happen to us? I felt such despair...

We had our Christmas in Sydney with the one aunty we had anything to do with. Our poor Nanna couldn't really understand what had happened. And poor Mum had all the responsibility of her. Dad's brother had no contact and was no support. We were basically on our own, apart from some nice friends.

The next year, 1968, was my first year in high school. It was a brand-new school, Oxley High School. I struggled with everything. There didn't seem to be any point to schoolwork — who would be interested in what I was doing now? I found it all very difficult and boring. My world had been turned upside down and all of this seemed trivial.

There was a bright spot though. We were having riding lessons again and this was a godsend. Our teacher this time was named Tex and I rode a pony called Sister. Tex's idea of a lesson was to take us for a ride around the streets of Tamworth and then into the hills nearby. I just loved it! However, I regularly came off Sister as she shied at everything! But it was so healing to be sitting on a horse and riding with a small group.

These lessons happened once a week and were a real highlight. We would arrive for our lesson and enter their little home – it was more like a hovel, dark, cluttered, and musty – and we would sit with Tex's wife Flo while Tex collected the horses from a nearby paddock. Flo seemed to watch TV all day, so we would sit with her and watch Bill and Ben from *The Flowerpot Men*, or sometimes *The Cisco Kid*! I loved being at that shabby place with the horse yards out the back. To me it was perfect!

Our life went on in a fashion. We kept on riding our bikes and climbing the hills behind us. I found such comfort taking off into the bush on my own. I would find a spot to sit and just think about Dad and ponder life. And during that year, we made friends with our new neighbours. The two girls were the same age as Sue and myself and we shared all our adventures in the bush – and sometimes set out on very long bike rides.

Meanwhile, our minister had encouraged Mum to start a local physical culture club, to give her an interest. She found a suitable teacher who was new to the area – and they had two girls our age! We all became firm friends with the Parks: a friendship that lasted throughout our teenage years and beyond. All these people helped to ease the grief at the time, but Mum was struggling.

Mum would sit and stare. She was so far away now... at times completely lost in herself. She told me in later years that she saw a psychiatrist as she had thought about committing suicide. Fortunately, she got through that time, but for the rest of her life lived with a deep sadness. She had already been a sad and faraway person at home – now it was worse. A good part of our mother died when Dad died. In many ways, we became the adults.

My school report that year was the worst one I had ever had. I had gone from being in the top ten of the class, to the lower half of the class. It wasn't surprising but it reinforced all my feelings of shame and unworthiness.

There was one highlight at school: swimming. I was working my way through the Life Saving levels. I received the Intermediate Star, still a treasured keepsake, and was preparing for the Bronze Medallion. Swimming was almost as healing as horse-riding. There is such a feeling of freedom in the water – the outside world recedes into the background and it's just you and the water.

And in that year, I stopped going to Sunday school. I had returned several weeks after Dad died, at the insistence of the minister, and my teacher made an example of me. I remember the words, 'Now look at Heather. Her father has just died, and God has talked to her and comforted her.' I was so embarrassed, but also, I was angry. The teacher wasn't talking TO me – she was talking ABOUT me! How did she know? I didn't hear God talk to me. NO ONE had talked to me and comforted me. No one! How could these people say these things!

I had never liked going to Sunday school, but it seemed to be something we did. Now I thought how false it all was. She was making up lies. Not one single person had talked to me and that included their God!

There was a lot to process. My father's death had sat inside me – a simmering wound. For 30 years it had festered away, unspoken about. The only time I had revisited it was when I was 32. I was pregnant with Emma, and Doug, Matt and I were travelling through Tamworth. I had previously asked Mum where I could find Dad's grave, but when I arrived at the lawn cemetery, I was so overwhelmed I sent Doug into the office for directions to the grave.

When we found it, I collapsed to the ground and cried and cried – there was my name on the plaque. So, it was real.... he really did die. I often had dreams that he just went away, and Mum had made up a story. But there it was. I wondered how we could have left him in the ground for so many years, seemingly forgotten. I didn't want to forget him – he deserved to be remembered – and I deserved to grieve.

But my trip to the cemetery at that time had only really opened the wound, it hadn't healed it.

Jannelle suggested I write a letter to my Dad. I read all of it out during my next session.

Dear Dad,

I've missed you so much.

Life hasn't been easy since you died – the emotional, physical and practical effects have been astounding. The grief has been woven through everything I do, and no doubt is the same for Sue and Ros.

You see, Mum went to pieces after you died, and she never really recovered. In many ways our childhood ended on the day you died. Many times, we had to be the parents as we were left without an adult.

I'm sad and angry that Mum handled the grieving as she did. Her remedy was to shut it all away and almost pretend you never existed. The impact of that has had lifelong consequences. No one asked us kids if we were okay. Sometimes I heard the adults talking – they would say things like 'Oh kids bounce back quickly,' as if we had just fallen over and then picked ourselves up again. How did they know I had bounced back? They were wrong... I felt dead inside...

I now need to properly grieve your passing. Dad, when you died my heart broke. I loved you so much – and I know you loved me. The grief has been in me ever since, but now I want to be set free. I want the darkness to end and the light to enter. Help me to see it – show me the way!

I want to be the person I was meant to be. This path to remembering has been a difficult one. Now,

I'm just really tired and I don't need to carry the sadness – or the anger – of how I was treated.

Goodbye Dad – you are always in my thoughts, and I want to think of you fondly from now on, not with the burden of sadness.

I will love you always!

Heather xxxx

The writing of the letter – and reading it aloud – was a very powerful exercise. The above is a condensed version. The session with Jannelle was emotional and exhausting, but so beneficial. I felt lighter – but there was more to do. I was so angry over how my sisters and I were treated throughout the grieving process. I needed to let that go.

Jannelle asked me to think about what I needed then to help me become me, and to do a meditation with my adult self for support. It proved to be key in moving on from the grief.

It went something like this.

As the adult, I told my young self about her dad's death without an audience – she spent time crying – and being held. Then I asked her to ask any questions or make any demands she needed to.

> YH: Can I see his body?
>
> **AH: Of course... how do you feel?**
>
> YH: I could say goodbye. I was allowed to cry. You were strong. You held me and showed respect.
>
> **AH: Has it made it any easier?**
>
> YH: Yes. To show the feelings. To be treated with dignity – there was no rush.
>
> **AH: There's nothing more important than you. Take all the time you want.**

After this meditation, I felt a huge burden had been lifted. My physical body felt so much lighter. I had a new spring in my step – a new confidence.

But there was a way to go...

AH: What did you need then to help you become you?

YH: I needed love, stability, a parent. I needed someone to listen to my school problems, to encourage me in my interests. Mainly, I needed love.

And so, gradually, I could accept my father's death more easily. The grief will always be there, but it now lives inside me in a more normal way. No one grieves in a perfect way, but to remove every reminder of a person who has died, to make them non-existent, is damaging beyond words.

A few years before Mum died, she was seeing a cardiologist. He asked her about heart issues in the family and she told him her husband had died at 44. He expressed how hard that must have been, but then said, 'How did your children cope? It must have been so hard for them.' She asked me if his death had affected me; she didn't seem to realise how much it had affected us. I was stunned! It wasn't even in her awareness!

I have read a very good book recently called *The Loss That Is Forever* by Maxine Harris. It's worth a read if the loss of a parent during childhood happened to you.

•●•

MY LEARNINGS

- Feelings of being unworthy were reinforced by the actions of the adults at the time of my father's death. I was not worthy enough to be hugged, or to have anyone talk to me about the tragedy.

- I learnt that my father's death was handled in the worst possible way, but I have continued to repair that damage and I now have a photo of Dad displayed in the house!

FOR THE READER

- Enduring the loss of a parent at an early age is a grief that is forever with you. However, it can be made easier if you are supported, comforted and allowed to talk about the deceased loved one.

- Keeping memories alive is very important – never let them fade.

- A child does not 'bounce back.' Grief is complex. Treat children who are grieving with dignity.

Chapter Seven

The Darkest Days Of All

'Kindness means caring — and caring is a special gift. It allows the child to be seen — even if for a fleeting moment. And that moment can sustain the soul until the next.'

— **Heather Binns**

Over the summer of 1968-1969, Mum announced that we were moving back to Sydney. I remember looking at her — staring in disbelief, trying to comprehend the words. Why would she want to leave our house? It was the last link to Dad. He'd bought the house, chosen it on his own. Why would we leave it?

It had only been a year since Dad had died and I didn't need my world to fall in again, but in that moment, it was feeling pretty dark. I was frowning, still taking in the words. My question was, 'Why?' I fought back tears. I loved country life, had a small circle of friends, I had my horse-riding, we had community support and I had the bush to sit in when I needed to. I also didn't want to leave Dad.

How could we just leave him there? Not only had every reminder of him disappeared, now we were moving away.

Mum said she would struggle to find work in Tamworth and there was more opportunity for all of us in the city. Really it was because she wanted to go back to the memories she had of those halcyon days in Sydney. I didn't blame her for that, and looking at her decision as an adult, I can see why she didn't want to stay in the house – and the town – where all the memories of Dad surrounded her. But it's never quite the same when you try to return to the past.

We moved in the winter of 1969. I was in Year 2 at high school and just 13. I'd had six months to adjust to the idea and resigned myself to it. We had lived in Tamworth for only three years and yet so much had happened. We had suffered the greatest of tragedies and I had fallen in love with country life.

On the final day before our move, I went walking in the bush behind our house. I loved the hillside leading to the lookout. It seemed to envelop our house and I always felt protected. There were so many places to explore, and I had my own secret spots. I sat there, feeling the ground under me, and looked at the distant hills. I vowed never to take country life for granted – to me it was a true gift to live in the open spaces – and one day I would return.

● ● ●

Mum had bought a house in Epping Avenue, Eastwood, however it would take another six months before we could move in. A friend's aunt had offered to have us stay with her, so we all squeezed into her house. I felt shell-shocked. I can still remember waking the first morning in this strange house and wanting to die. But we were all struggling. Sometimes Mum and Ros would fight, and Mum would lose it completely and start throwing things. It's scary when the adult loses it and, now I'm an adult myself, I can understand that Mum – and all of us – were under extreme stress.

Once again, I was a new girl. The years at Cheltenham Girls High School were possibly the most depressing time of my childhood. The school was way ahead in work compared to Oxley High School and it was stuffy and unfriendly. I felt overwhelmed and I couldn't keep up. I had no idea what they were talking about in most of the subjects.

I was back with my friend, Kath – and very happy I had her to help me – but some of the girls in her group didn't like me from the start. I guess I was an easy target: quiet and timid.

As those years went on, I did make a few friends… or acquaintances, however, I stayed loyal to Kath and sat with her and her group for lunch. These girls had either ignored or bullied me from when I first arrived at the school and they would laugh in front of me at my nervous tic, which had developed since the move. When anyone asked about my dad, I felt so embarrassed and ashamed that I didn't have a father. In those days it was very unusual to be in a single parent family.

I had never been bullied until then. For anyone who has been bullied, you know what it is like.

These girls didn't bully me every day – they did it intermittently. I never knew when it was coming. But I lived in fear of them each day. I was 'lesser.' It reinforced all those old thought highways in the brain. I felt humiliated, my confidence was at zero, I was unimportant, boring, different and I didn't belong.

So, why did I put up with it? Why didn't I just go and find someone else? I was loyal to my childhood friend, Kath. This was the group of friends she had found when I left Sydney for Tamworth. I had come back into her world, and she had welcomed me. In my brain, if I found some other group to be with, I would be abandoning her as well. I thought it was best to put up with this. There were times when she did defend me against these girls, but there were other times when she was absent, and they were able to put the boot in.

Despite my fear I would think to myself, 'You stupid girls, you are so pampered, worrying about childish things when I have adult worries to contend with.'

Despite my troubles at school, it was a relief to move into our permanent home. Mum had gone to a refresher course and had started work. Things were looking up! But the house, or rather the people in it, were sad. There was an emptiness, a void, that could not be filled, even though my sisters and I laughed a lot. We all loved music and the latest songs were always playing on the radio at home. Music was very much a healing therapy and an escape. It filled the air and helped to disguise that emptiness.

So, this became our new normal – and normal for me was feeling ever so lonely. We were moving further and further on without Dad, and the new life, no matter how happy it could sound, was permeated with sadness.

On a brighter note, Mum was very good to me. She let me have riding lessons as she knew how much they meant to me. I was also interested in drawing, so she bought me the Walter T Foster book on how to draw horses. This book became well-worn. I would spend hours in my room drawing, which I found very comforting. I kept the book and still have it in my box of precious things. Drawing was therapeutic for me.

The riding lessons were like a true riding school where we rode around an arena for an hour while the teacher screamed commands at us. While it wasn't ideal, it gave me a vital link back to country life, but it was nothing like our rides with Tex. I missed those so much – and I missed Tex and our little group of riders.

Despite being screamed at, I chose to continue these lessons, rather than give them up when money was scarce. Mum gave me a choice: clothes or riding lessons. The choice was easy – I went without new clothes. I think I had my school uniform and one or two home outfits!

Mum really did try hard to provide for us and make our new life comfortable, but she had limited funds. She had a small superannuation pension from Dad, but it was a small amount considering his early death. Dad's Will took years to finalise as the files were lost for some time. They would have stayed lost had a friend of Mum's not enquired. Mum had trustingly waited for over three years.

During those years, Mum borrowed money at a high rate of interest and that was the start of her financial demise.

She was never a good money manager and was an easy source of prey for con men. In fact, she got into financial difficulty quickly but told us we weren't to say anything to anyone about our money situation. This was drummed into us regularly. It was our family secret.

We became part of the cover up – the conspiracy. We had to play the game. We were forced to present to the outside world that all was okay, when we were living a lie.

Mum was trying to maintain to everyone else that we were a comfortable middle-class family, yet there were times when there was no food in the cupboards. We ate lots of toast.

She could not let her friends from the old days know – she was way too proud – but pride comes at a price. She put so much energy into obsessing over this secret and worrying about money. She would lay awake all night, yet she would not contact a charity organisation or ask a friend for help.

All these events reinforced her negative mindset which she passed on to us. We were constantly told we must listen to the authorities and not question, but worse, that we weren't as important as others and that we suffered from 'The Crawford's Bad Luck.'

In other words, we were victims and we had no voice – that was our lot in life. Others were more important and we needed to just accept that we were lesser.

If we complained, or had a worry, we were told that we wouldn't know what worries were. We thought this was normal. We assumed it was the truth, but these constant thoughts take such a toll.

The three of us worried desperately about Mum's wellbeing. She was all we had. Without her, we would be orphans, with no family to look after us. The focus on Mum left no space for us to develop the normal teenage traits. We had adult problems to deal with – the lack of money became our worry as well, and her sad and anxious ways dominated our thoughts. We never caused a minute's worry to her, we just wanted her to be happy.

You don't think these details are doing damage, but they are. You become consumed in these series of worries even if you appear to be fine. Trying to constantly fix someone, to try and make them happy, takes a toll. You know you can't fix it, but it doesn't stop you from constantly worrying about it.

And we did have many happy moments – it wasn't all doom and gloom! I had my friend Kath, and we were fortunate to have our friends from the country, the Parks, living in Sydney. We would get together and laugh and laugh. It was a wonderful tonic and I thank them so much for being there. We had country friends visit in school holidays. There were trips to the beach, pool, shopping centres and the city.

There were many things to be thankful for, but the purpose of this study of the past was to see what happened in those teenage years and how it had impacted on me.

I started to gain weight in those years. I had always been tiny but now I was eating way too much. Even though our food cupboards were often sparse, I found enough to eat. It may have been toast but I consumed huge amounts! I was always hungry – trying to fill the hole inside me. I often felt like I was odd.

The world did seem scary, and Mum kept reinforcing to us that, indeed, it was! I started to sit on the lounge a lot and watch TV as the lounge was safe – I could switch off and not be afraid. Maybe I just sat there in shock as I couldn't bear my new life. It was my way of mourning.

In the next session with Jannelle we talked about the weight gain and my time sitting on the lounge. I was transported back to that 14-year-old and started to sob. It was a far cry from the girl who would head off into the bush for hours, or who would bike ride or swim. I just sat.

I talked to my child self after the session.

> **AH: We've just seen Jannelle. You were surprised at your emotion over the emptiness you feel.**
>
> YH: Yes, it was a shock – the emptiness – I fill it up with food, sleep, anxiety and unattainable dreams.
>
> **AH: So, it's like a big doughnut hole. What did you need to fill it?**
>
> YH: I guess warmth, things to do, friends, books etc.
>
> **AH: But those things are doing things – what is it you really needed?**
>
> YH: ...LOVE

Love... it seems so hard to come by. The eating was a coping mechanism and then it became a habit later in life. Some people choose alcohol or drugs – I chose food. When I am stressed or tired, food is still my drug of choice.

School was still a daily challenge. We had a new headmistress, Miss Smith. She was as severe as they came. Dress lengths were measured, the deepest blue of sock colour was insisted upon – too bad if they faded in the wash – and if you forgot your hat, you were on detention.

In the four years I was there, not one teacher knew me. I was so quiet, and just tried to get through the day, so I spent a lot of time trying to be invisible. My reports each year said the same thing. I was amazed they could write about me as they didn't even know my name… 'Heather could try harder. She should show more interest. She can do better. She is too quiet.'

The reports would infuriate me. Even then I shed tears. I felt I tried as hard as I could. Most weekends were spent doing homework. How much harder could I try? And just because I was quiet didn't mean I wasn't interested. Why do you get punished for being quiet?

I had been writing each day in my God book – this is one of the conversations we had.

> *God, the school reports – they always make me cry.*
>
> **One day they won't. So much of your life has been based on how you perceived yourself then. You need to change your way of thinking and realise you did so well under the circumstances. Don't measure yourself on some silly value system. Everyone is worthy – you all gauge yourselves in such a narrow**

way. You were just fine then. These people wrote without thought. Feel my love – it's more powerful than those words.

These writings helped me heal, but the healing was slow.

In the early 70s, most students left school after the School Certificate in Year 4 (now known as Year 10) and only the 'bright' ones went on. However, I was legally too young to leave, so I stayed on for Year 5 – which is now known as Year 11.

Looking back now, I realise I was very depressed, but there was a ray of light that year – sport! The school was considering whether horse-riding could be included as a sport for Year 11. I was so excited! I went with some other girls to approach Miss Smith to ask her permission. I couldn't believe she said yes! My Thursdays became a ray of sunshine. We were going to ride at Mrs Batchelor's riding school. Pearl Batchelor founded Riding for the Disabled the same year and was eventually awarded the Order of Australia medal for her services to the community.

> She was one of the Kind Ladies. Her kindness towards me kept me going.

Spending time with Mrs Batchelor was as rewarding as riding the horses! I developed quite a rapport with her.

She would greet me with a hug and was always cheery. **She was one of the Kind Ladies. Her kindness towards me kept me going.**

Each Thursday was like 'tonic day' and it made school life bearable that year.

There was so much anger within me still. I needed to continue writing about these school years.

MY LEARNINGS

- I had entered adolescence at the same time I suffered two major life stresses. I was already traumatised. It was like starting the marathon run to adulthood with a leg missing. It was important for me to see that I had been impacted before this crucial stage in life even began.

- A few nasty comments from school 'friends' and negative comments from teachers can be subconsciously carried through the rest of your life. I truly thought I was unpopular, ugly and not very smart.

- I was so lucky to have my sisters to share this time with. We are the only three who will ever truly understand what it was like.

MY LEARNINGS

- I perceived the world as scary and dark. I was 'lesser.' I could have no opinion.

- I sought comfort by being creative, being the clown and eating.

- I felt responsible for my mother's happiness, but I couldn't fix it.

- Lack of money was a well-kept family secret but dominated our lives.

FOR THE READER

- The teenage years are often the hardest for both the parent and teenager. If your family has gone through a trauma, it's important to understand that your teenager is suffering, even if it doesn't seem so. Positive support is essential.

- If you suffered during the teenage years, be aware that these years can have a huge impact on the rest of your life. Revisit those years with a professional if you need to.

Chapter Eight

The Invisible Girl

'Our place of safety eventually turns against us. What we thought was our salvation is now our torment. The longer we stay there, the further we recede – invisible to the world – and to ourselves.'

— **Heather Binns**

I spent a lot of time with Jannelle going over the teenage years. I had pulled out all my reports, photos and school magazines. The reports upset me greatly – it was the same all through high school: 'Heather is not trying, she is too quiet, she doesn't show interest, she could do better, she could try harder.'

Jannelle suggested I write a letter to the teachers at the school. It was a very angry letter.

To all the awful teachers,

Did you ever really see me? Did you see the pain in my eyes? I was grieving so much for my Dad. I tried hard to smile when I was dying inside. But no one noticed or cared. And I didn't care about the work – what was the point? My life had ended at 11. You just kicked me when I was down with your harsh words.

Fancy saying I needed to develop a more vital interest. I was still grieving – are you all stupid? I had no energy to give. I held my emotions in all those years. I worried about my Mum. You had no idea.

You judged me by my grades and my quietness. Does that mean a lack of interest? I think I did exceptionally well considering my depressed state and the fact I was a year younger than most of the others, AND the fact that NO ONE – and I mean NO ONE – was watching out for me.

Do you know how much your careless words hurt me? I'm not going to be a victim of them anymore, I've thrown your opinions away. I'm finding my confidence and strength. I'm free to be me...

Heather

• ● •

I thought I had finished with the teenage years, but it still hurt. I needed to stay at this stage longer. There was more writing to be done.

What was it about the reports that made me so angry – why was I so hurt? Why had it had such an impact on me? Why did it enrage me? What did I feel?

Once again, I was sitting on my bed crying. Those reports had sat packed away for almost 30 years, but now it was important to dig deep and pull apart the rage.

I saw myself then as a quiet, law-abiding student who did their homework on time and sat in class, never making a fuss. The teachers saw me as disinterested, too quiet and thought I could try harder.

What were they seeing?

And then it came to me…

They were seeing a shut-down human, yet they didn't recognise me as that. They came to the wrong conclusion – I was shut down rather than disinterested. I was coping the only way I knew how.

> They were seeing a shut-down human, yet they didn't recognise me as that.

In fact, you could say they were asking me to run a race and couldn't see my broken leg, so they assumed I wasn't trying hard enough.

I was judged by a flawed system – flawed in so many ways. I

needed a helping hand, rather than a punishment. I was misjudged as being disinterested and quiet; those labels were negatives. There wasn't one positive.

I was invisible and my pain and struggles were invisible. Now I was crying for every single student who had been judged by a harsh and flawed system. I was crying for humanity, for the narrow-minded view society takes on getting children through the education system. I was crying for my soul and for theirs.

Where is the kindness, where is the empathy? Adults and teachers need to see, to REALLY see, the human in front of them. Adolescence can be the make-or-break years and careless words written on paper seep into your brain to work on the highways in your mind.

This was what my anger was about. I went back over my reports, school magazines and any other memories of that time. I needed to leave that stage with a feeling of peace. I hadn't found it. I wrote again to my child self.

> **AH: You're back to your reports again. You are still angry.**
>
> YH: My final report said I shouldn't be satisfied with the result. Why? Why shouldn't I? I didn't fail anything! In fact, I didn't get below 60 percent in anything – even maths! I always ranked in the top half of my year. What did they hope to achieve by saying that?
>
> **AH: I don't know. I guess the teachers were locked into a system. Schools were always promoting**

themselves. They needed the students to make them look good. Now you are looking at photos from a Year 4 formal. Why? I can feel you are angry.

YH: Look at that girl in the dance picture. I dreamt of being that beautiful and confident. I felt so inferior, unnoticed. I just thought that was my lot. I didn't make the grade – never quite good enough – and I was unnoticed because I wasn't worth noticing so I just didn't think I was capable of much.

AH: You had strength and courage.

YH: I wasn't strong. I was terrified!

AH: Yes, you were! You found ways to cope – all on your own!

YH: In that magazine, they were talking about how many of the senior girls drove cars to school. We couldn't even afford new shoes! My shoes had a big crack in the sole – but I told Mum they would be okay until I left school. On rainy days my foot would be wet all day!

AH: And that shows strength! You managed to keep on going with discomfort to avoid an extra cost. It also shows maturity and responsibility. Well done!

Strength! I hadn't ever thought I had strength. I wrote in my God book about this:

> *God, I don't see myself as having strength, I just see myself as this timid little girl.*

Heather you are so strong! Picture your inner strength – like a beacon on a rock – and focus on it. You'll be amazed at how it will help. Because in there you will find me helping you all the way. I'll never leave you alone. I will always look after you! I love you! Remember – there is nothing to fear!

These words helped so much. I had never allowed myself to think that I had strength and courage – but still I argued the point with God.

> *God, how can I be strong? Here I am spending my days on the bed while others are out working or just getting on with it! (At this point I think God was rolling his eyes in despair!)*

Heather why are you still devaluing what you are doing! Do you know how many people would be brave enough to do an in-depth study of themselves? To be so open? To let their defences down? You are amazing!

If more people would just stop and listen, the world would be a better place. Take those qualities you have of courage and strength. Own them! You deserve them. You earnt them the minute you were born. You knew then that there is nothing to fear.

I started to feel the changes inside me. Until now I had just identified the negative feelings – I had mapped out the highways in my brain, the highways of fear, grief, unworthiness, being lesser, being shamed, etc. Now, there were new roads springing up. The road of courage and the road of strength. They may have just been dirt tracks, but I could now see them on the map. I could feel a turning point.

I was finally ready to move on from school and into my working years.

I found there was some deep regret over my career choice. I didn't understand why. In the 1970s, women in general weren't encouraged to focus on a career. The expectation was that they would be a teacher, secretary or nurse and then leave work when they got married. I didn't really mind being a secretary. In fact, it was wise advice from Mum. I easily found work, started saving money and travelled.

So, what was buried in there that I hadn't found?

I had a conversation with my child self:

> YH: Why did Mum encourage all of us to be secretaries? I wanted to do something creative, like interior design.
>
> **AH: Your Mum knew that having skills in an area that was in demand was a good way to start. Yes, it was a safe option. But you didn't really have much choice. You needed to be earning your own money as soon as you could.**
>
> YH: I guess so.

AH: There's more to this isn't there. I can feel it. Can you talk more about it?

YH: Well, it was just so 'safe.' Mum drummed into us that the world was a scary place. If we didn't do the right thing, the authorities would punish us.

AH: Why is that?

YH: Mum told us that we weren't as good as other people, and to put others before ourselves. She said bad things happen — it's just how it is for us — and we have to learn to live with it. We just drew the 'loser' card in life. It's just how it is. We need to take a safe path in life.

AH: You know now it isn't true.

YH: But then it was true!

AH: So, you're safe in that box but not happy.

YH: No. Mum always said, magic doesn't happen at our house.

AH: What do you think will happen to you if you jump out of the box?

YH: I'LL LIVE.

AH: What's stopping you?

YH: FEAR.

The Invisible Girl

I had identified what it was – the regret was not with the career choice – it was with my programmed mindset. I was 44 and still programmed from my teenage years. It was all in there, mixed up with the grief and the loneliness and deeply-buried memories of frightening times in babyhood.

I sat there on the bed and thought, 'What an awful mess I am!' All the ingredients were there. No wonder I'd had a breakdown! I was surprised I'd got to my 40s before it all started to unravel.

Again, I wrote in my God book.

> *God, I feel like I've really messed up my career. I'm content with being a mum, but the kids will be independent in a few years – what then? Am I just grieving lost opportunities?*
>
> **Are you? Heather, your greatest barrier is fear – let it down! I'll say it over and over. You have many, many talents – one of the greatest is the value you put on your children. See why you had the childhood experiences you did? So you could learn – you have great understanding. I've said it before: the value you put on your family and the understanding you have that your children are individuals with their own soul plan will help them immensely.**
>
> **Your children are the next generation, and you are showing them the way – leading them to greater understanding. You KNOW that love is all that matters – let the fear go! You are providing a turning point for the future. Your children are growing up with wisdom – they know they are totally loved – so value your career.**
>
> *Wow God! Thank you! That makes me cry!*

• ● •

It was around this time in my therapy that I sensed something significant had happened to me as a baby. Even though I had moved past the baby years, something was niggling at me. At this point, I didn't know the truth of what had happened, which took many more years to come out, but even then I had a sense that there was more. I wrote to God about it.

God, I was rejected way back, wasn't I?

Yes.

All this grief is not just about Dad – something happened when I was really young. I was scared then that I'd be ridiculed if I showed emotion. Whatever happened shamed me. It goes way back to babyhood, as a newborn. With Mum, there is a huge barrier, like I'm 'on guard.'

Yes, that's right.

Well, if this rejection is in me, how do I get it out?

You've done well to be able to trace your feelings. It means you must never forget how special you are. You are WORTHY. Keep telling yourself that. You know I'm always here. You need to get this Heather. You need energy to do what you have to do, and you CAN do it! Don't let this unworthiness win. You weren't the problem. Your mum has many issues to deal with. You've tried to make your mother happy all your life. You cannot do it for her!

But I feel sad and angry. What do I do about my anger? How do I get over never having these emotional needs met?

Well, why would you want to hang onto it? Just give it up! You know I'm with you. I will meet your every need, I'll hold you when you cry, I'll listen to your problems, I'll laugh with you, I'll calm your fears, I'll tell you how special you are. Over and over and over, I'll help guide you and help you to remember who you really are. I'll comfort you, I'll talk to you, I'll be with you – through everything and everywhere – forever and ever, always, in life after life. There is nothing to fear, so there is nothing to feel unworthy about. You are extra special: you listened and found me. You have many things to do – now go and start.

Wow! Thank you, God – you make me feel much better.

Heather, your parents were only human and came to you with all their wounds. Forgive them for that – sure, grieve it – but don't hold it within you. Let it go.

This writing helped me so much, not only to delve deeper as new awareness came to me, but also to move through the pain, to shift the anger within me. With each conversation I felt another part of me come alive.

It was finally time to do the meditation at the end of the adolescent years. This had been a really tough stage – and it was the final meditation where you bring all the stages together.

While it is a guided meditation, by this stage in my therapy I was doing it my own way. I would start with the meditation and then see what happened, rather than trying to focus on the words guiding me.

I started in a corridor as my adult self, and I went to each door to greet all the different stages. First, I picked up my teenage self and she looked so much happier. Next was my school age self, then the pre-schooler, toddler and baby.

There was lots of laughter as we greeted each other, but as I opened the door to the baby it was different. I opened the door to a paddock with a beautiful tree in the middle of it. The baby was in a pram under the tree, the sun was shining and there were little birds everywhere.

Once again, the tears rolled, but this time because it was so beautiful! She was surrounded by love and exactly where she belonged – not in the dark room. She was part of the connection of all things, very loved, very special. She was at peace.

I was so happy to have this image as it symbolised that all the work I had been doing was having such a positive effect. I was now seeing the parts of me in a different way. I was so much happier. I was getting my needs met, being listened to and being loved.

The teenage years were becoming much less significant in my head. I had worked through anger and grief. All this analysis was very worthwhile.

MY LEARNINGS

- I felt alone and unsupported much of the time. These years were my first experience of depression.

- I was surprised at the anger towards the teachers. For me to heal I needed to get that anger out.

- In the end, I think I did really well during adolescence, considering the circumstances.

- I realise that teenagers need so much to hear positives, not negatives.

- I sensed there was more to my time as a baby – that there was some deep-seated trauma.

FOR THE READER

- If you are a teenager and struggling, please reach out to someone — there is the Kids Helpline in Australia: https://kidshelpline.com.au/teens. There should be an organisation in the country you are living in. Have a look online.

- If you are the parent of a teenager, watch your child for signs of depression and spend as much time talking to them as you can. I know teenage boys often just grunt — but there are times when they want to talk!

- For high school teachers, school reports need at least one positive, even if the results aren't great.

- If you have similar memories of teenage years, I suggest therapy — and know that you are perfect just as you are!

Chapter Nine

Change Creates Chaos

'Isn't that how falling in love so often works? Some stranger appears out of nowhere and becomes a fixed star in your universe.'

— **Kate Bolick**

After leaving school, I spent a year at TAFE learning all areas of secretarial work and then worked in the Sydney CBD for two years which opened up a whole new world for me – then we tired of the city.

Ros, Sue and I wanted to move back to the country, so we all moved, Mum included, to Lismore on the far north coast of NSW. What a relief to get to the country again! I loved looking at the open space around me – all the green rolling hills, and the ocean a short drive away. I didn't miss the city at all! It was like I could finally breathe out again after so many years. There was a sense of ease – everyone was so laid back after the hectic city life.

I worked with a great group of girls, and we socialised regularly, but there was something missing. It was a sense of belonging. Had I really belonged anywhere? I felt like

I had been transient all my life – not just physically – but I felt like I didn't truly belong anywhere. What did I mean by that? I didn't really know then.

•●•

At the end of 1976, there was an ad in the paper for a meeting to form a bushwalking club. This was something that appealed. I thought about all those times I had sat in the bush for comfort when I was younger. I loved the idea of walking and camping in the bush.

For all the dark moments of the previous six years in the city, I was about to become part of something where I felt like I truly belonged: The Northern Rivers Bushwalkers Club. What was it about this group that gave that sense of belonging? Most of us were new to the area, we were in our 20s, we all had an appreciation for the environment… but there was more. It was like a magic wand had been waved and there was a spark as if we had been waiting all our lives to meet up.

Over the next seven years we shared so many adventures. We walked, camped, abseiled, kayaked, explored caves, rode airbeds down rapids… but most of all, we laughed. We were like one big family. Here were the brothers, sisters, cousins etc. that I had been missing. We were so comfortable in each other's company. We socialised nearly every weekend when we weren't out visiting some wonder of the natural world.

GREAT CAMPFIRE - GREAT FRIENDS!
c. Roger Sheppeard

So why did I feel so comfortable? What makes those times feel so close to my heart? I think it was because I was seen! I had felt I was invisible for most of my life. I was probably the closest to my true self in those times.

There was no judgement, just laughter. It didn't matter how much money I had, what I did or what I looked like, we were there for the friendship and fun.

We had a 40-year reunion a few years back, and it was wonderful to feel that same comfortable feeling. I think in some ways we are always searching for that sense of belonging that I found with this group.

Apart from friendships, there were some romances, some of which led to lifelong partnerships. I was in that category. It was in this group that I met Doug. He had finished his forestry degree and was at his first job, living in a small town called Urbenville. He heard about the club from his work colleague and came along.

I didn't meet Doug until he'd been in the group for a while, but my first impression was that he felt familiar. There was something about him. I was drawn to his eyes, and I loved his quiet way and was amazed by his knowledge of the plants and animals. He would come to our monthly meetings looking like he'd just crawled out of the forest – he was normally barefoot – and wore an old green cardigan that had been patched and patched!

He was certainly different from the average person. I admired his intelligence and earthiness. But it was the familiarity, the chemistry, his whole manner. It was like I knew him before I even knew him! I had a moment of just knowing – knowing that this was the person I had to spend my life with.

I had fallen in love.

It was like finding the missing piece of the jigsaw puzzle – but instead of a puzzle it was a missing piece of me!

I was so happy he felt the same way!

We did six months of travelling. We trekked in South America, visited Machu Picchu, explored glaciers in the Andes, became very ill in the jungles of Bolivia and endured a long, cramped train ride through the Atacama Desert – just to name a few adventures.

We finally married in 1983 and I moved to Eden, on the NSW south coast, where Doug had started a new job. It was so hard to leave family and friends, but my heart was elsewhere, so I finished work and off I went to start a new life. Eden felt very wild and remote, and I loved it! I got to know people quickly and enjoyed the short time we had there.

During the years living on the north coast, Sue and I lived with Mum, while Ros moved out. Sue and I had stayed at home way longer than we intended, but we felt it was the right thing to do as Mum had been quite depressed for several years. We couldn't stay forever, but we worried constantly. Since I was 11, I had worried about Mum.

While I felt relief at moving away, I still worried and felt guilty. It was the same feeling you might have if you have a night or two away and leave your young children with their grandparents. The worry is always there in the back of your mind.

When you have a parent on their own, you naturally worry about them, but this was more. My wish was always for her to be happy, and it weighed heavily on me that she never was. I couldn't change it, but all the same I couldn't let it go.

We were only in Eden for 18 months as Doug moved to another job in Wauchope, on the mid north coast of NSW. We thought we would be there forever — but that didn't happen.

Our son Matt arrived in 1986, and daughter Emma in 1989. I always wanted to be a mother and I became fully absorbed in these two beautiful children. However, Emma's birth had been full of drama (I had nearly died!) and when she was just six weeks old, we were moving again.

Doug had been pressured by Forestry management to move to Sydney. Sydney! The very place I wanted to stay out of. But in the end, we had no choice, so off we went, moving to a house on a busy road because it was all we could afford.

The days could be lonely as a mother of a toddler and baby, and I knew no one in Sydney except my childhood friend Kath. It was so good to have her there.

Mum stayed with us for four months and I was very grateful to her. She was an amazing help and if it wasn't for her,

I would have certainly been admitted to hospital. I had flashbacks to Emma's birth each night, and I had a baby that did not sleep! What I realise now is that I had PTSD and postnatal depression. I should have been seeking help – but I wouldn't have known where to go.

Mum was a different person in her relationship to her grandchildren. She was gentle, affectionate and understanding. They adored her. I was so happy to see it. They gave her a new lease on life – a reason to live – and in return she gave them so much love.

I had no idea that Doug's new job involved so much time away. He would be gone for two weeks at a time – there were no mobile phones then – and when he came home, he struggled to settle into family life and we would argue.

He would eventually settle and was good with the kids, built cubby houses, played games, changed nappies etc. It was the transition period from the two lives he was living that was difficult. It was taking a toll on our marriage.

Once again, I pushed myself out to meet people, and when the kids were older, times were better. I made many good friends, but I hated where we lived. I couldn't stand the busy road. We spent so much time renovating the house when we could afford it and Doug did an amazing job.

But even when all the house was done, I wasn't happy. I started to wake at three in the morning feeling utter despair. I was very busy: I was working part-time, involved with the school, making craft and selling it at the markets, and enjoying time with friends, but I continued to struggle living in the city. I told Doug I was sorry that I'd made him renovate the house. I realised that it didn't matter what we did to it – it was still right there on the busy road.

I longed to have space around me, not to hear traffic all night. I broke down and told Doug I couldn't do it anymore. I had to get out of the city as it was all too much. I had tried hard for seven years but there was no way I could live the rest of my life there.

Doug could see the state I was in and told me he would see if there were any jobs in the country. He was happy with his work and had good friends in his work colleagues, but his job was in doubt as the department was going through a major restructure.

That made all the difference to me as I could finally see a way out. I had felt helpless about the situation as I'd had no choice about where we lived. Doug earnt the money and I had chosen to be a stay-at-home mum. It was my career. In the 13 years of marriage, we had moved three times, built one house and renovated another. I had spent so much time settling into the new places and building a network. I was good at it. I would push myself to go out and be the new girl everywhere. I'd had enough, but I could do it one more time if it meant escaping the city.

I learnt that sometimes no amount of positivity and soldiering on can work if deep down your soul is so unhappy. In fact, you are just putting a band-aid on the problem while it continues to fester away.

About two months after my meltdown, Doug told me there was a job in Coffs Harbour, but before he applied for it, I had to be absolutely sure it was what I wanted. I had no doubts for myself, but my kids! Matt was nine – did I want to pull him away from his friends? I agonised over whether it was the right thing to do, and we all talked about it together. Both kids agreed they wanted to go... but I knew they didn't really know what they were agreeing to.

> I learnt that sometimes no amount of positivity and soldiering on can work if deep down your soul is so unhappy.

Each night, I hoped something would present itself so that I was sure it was the right decision. Nothing did – until two nights before the applications closed. That night I dreamt of a bedroom that opened onto a balcony. The breeze was blowing in gently and I could hear the ocean in the distance. I knew in the morning Doug had to apply.

We moved to Coffs Harbour at the end of 1996 into the house I had dreamt about. The bedroom where I was doing the Study of Myself was the bedroom in my dream. But it was never my dream house. It was somehow wrong. Yet it ticked all the boxes of our requirement in a family house, even though we had put ourselves in more debt!

Despite some ups and downs, we settled into Coffs Harbour. I loved the clean air and open space. I could see glimpses of the ocean and hear it, and I could drive around with ease and not get caught up in traffic. I had no regrets!

Yet three years after our move I was falling apart in the 'dream bedroom' and our relationship was stretched to breaking point.

During my therapy, Doug realised he'd been in a state of depression since our move to Coffs Harbour, so we were both down – although for different reasons. He didn't want to do anything except be at home and tend to his garden and plants. He had been off in his own little world for some time. Even camping with the kids with friends from bushwalking days didn't inspire him.

He was very distant from us. I felt like the kids and I were a chore to him. He preferred to be in his own little world.

Because of the therapy, I was gradually changing. I wasn't the person he had married 17 years previously. It was hard for him to adapt. I had gained more wisdom in that dark year of 2000 than I had in a lifetime! There were tears and anger, but there was also lots of talking – and the key to resolving our troubles was that we didn't lay blame. We just recognised we both had a different focus, and the question was, could we sort it out and stay together?

For almost two years we trod this rocky road. In my therapy, I came to realise that I had thought of myself as 'lesser' than Doug. I also had anger towards him that was really anger directed to my Dad. I was angry he died. There was part of me that wanted Doug to take the place of my Dad. That is, in some ways I was still 11 years old.

Manoeuvring through all these mixed-up emotions was hard work. It involved lots of writing, some exhausting sessions with Jannelle, and many, many talks with Doug.

But I wasn't the only one at fault, and we both had to take responsibility for where we had ended up.

We had to get it sorted. We had a 13-year-old and an 11-year-old. They, of course, were our most important focus. There had been so much sadness. One day I said to Doug that I was okay if he decided he wanted to opt out of our relationship. I just wanted all the sadness to end and for both of us to be happy. I told him to go outside and just think about what he really wanted. I didn't want to deny him freedom if he felt pressured by family demands. I was strong enough at that point to deal with whatever decision he made.

He came back inside later on and said he'd be lost without us and would do whatever it took to make changes. I was so relieved, because despite all the sadness, we had never stopped loving each other.

But that was only the start of the long road back to repairing our relationship. No matter what, there was no way I was going to let the kids suffer. They always deserved two parents with them. I'd been through the loss of a parent – they weren't going to suffer the same.

I would work through everything, and if Doug and I couldn't fix certain things, well, we could call a truce. If anyone was going to suffer it was us – not our kids.

My emotions would wax and wane. There was so much anger inside and it had to come out. The anger wasn't just about my Dad dying, I was angry at myself for living like I had. I had somehow seen Doug as a father figure who would look after me and when it started to unravel

— when I separated Dad from Doug — I was so confused. But I was also becoming so much stronger. I realised that some parts of me had stayed 11 years old. Now that I was reclaiming myself, I had a new outlook.

Doug was also working through his own depression and attitude towards everything. I'd had Doug up on a pedestal. I spent time drawing diagrams of our family as stick figures. The kids and I were always drawn quite small and Doug was much bigger. Sometimes I drew him in his own bubble and we were outside knocking on the door. I was hoping that one day I would draw us all together — and smiling.

I was becoming a different person and Doug was running to keep up, as well as dealing with his own issues. Now I was making so many more demands on him. I kept moving forward, he would finally catch up — then I moved again!

But what kept us together through it all were our talks, and there was something else I had in my toolkit — my writing. I would go to my God book regularly.

> *God, can you help me? What is it about Doug? What is it about his burning passion/obsession that I, the kids and other things get in the way of?*
>
> **Doug loves his plants — they are very connected, and you know that. They are connected so well that sometimes people are secondary. But Heather, he met you. You are very special to him. Do you know why he met you? You have an incredible talent for understanding people — for being so aware — and he needed that. He needs to learn things from you, even though he doesn't realise that.**

You were MEANT to meet – it was no accident! You seem poles apart, but you both have gifts to give each other. Doug's has been to make you more self-sufficient by bringing you to this crisis. Yours has been to help Doug to become softer, more understanding. In a sense, you're a perfect combination, but I know you don't see that.

Heather, it's a hard road and your strength is amazing. There is so much love. You both needed to release that anger. Hang on and ride out the storm. I love you and there is nothing to fear!

I read out the above to Doug and it brought tears to his eyes. He started to feel and understand, rather than go into defence mode – he was so amazed by the kind words of wisdom.

I had told Doug early on about my writings. At first, I thought he may scoff at it. I didn't really care if he did, but he didn't. He liked my version of God; to him it was a far better and more useful version than the religious model. These writings really helped us to get through the dark days of our relationship.

We used to discuss what it really may be – was it a hidden part of myself? Are we all born with this part and it is only accessed by some? Was it something that floated around unseen, some sort of hidden energy? My mind would wonder about all the possibilities, but really it didn't matter what it actually was. I was just so happy to find it!

What I realise now when I look back on our troubles is that it just took time. When you become aware of something it doesn't automatically get fixed. You are viewing life through new eyes and it can be frightening, but as life went on we started to settle into a new way of being together.

> When you become aware of something it doesn't automatically get fixed. You are viewing life through new eyes and it can be frightening…

Doug looks back now and has regrets. He realises how short a time we have our children with us and how important family is. He calls them his 'arsehole days.' Despite these times, our family has always been close-knit, and we just so enjoy being in each other's company.

I tell him not to regret it. We did the best we could as parents and partners and I know our kids think we did pretty well!

It took three to four years to find peace with each other, to sort out all the changes – and in our case, we wanted it to work. Talking it out was a real key to our progress.

●●●

MY LEARNINGS

- I learnt how my father's death had impacted on my mental/emotional health. I looked and acted like a perfectly normal, responsible adult – but underneath I wanted my partner to meet my 11-year-old needs.

- I was unaware my anger towards Doug was mixed up with anger towards my father for dying.

- Having a new awareness doesn't mean the problem is automatically fixed – it takes time.

FOR THE READER

- Using the power of positivity can be a huge help, but sometimes it becomes a barrier. It can be a band-aid solution. Don't ignore what's underneath.

- The path to becoming yourself can be littered with obstacles. It can create chaos in a relationship. But once you start on that path you can't go back – you can't just return to the old you. It's a matter of dealing with each change in the best way you can. That may mean separating from your partner, depending on the issues. Or it may be that you need to work through it. Just remember – it takes time!

Chapter Ten

It's All An Illusion!

'If we have not found heaven within, it is a certainty we will not find it without.'

— Henry Miller

I thought I was having therapy to explore my past, but I soon found out I was having way more than therapy – I was having a spiritual awakening!

After my first 'white light' moment, everything changed. Not only was I writing to this light which I named God, I was meditating and resting, and during this time my sixth sense was heightened. I had always had psychic moments, but this was on a different level.

It was like I opened a door to the real world and everything as we knew it was just an illusion. That's how I saw it; or you could say that our view of the world is like the tip of the iceberg — there is so much more underneath, but we never see it.

Everything looked different, clearer. But apart from that, everything was connected. I would sit on my bed and marvel at the communication going on outside my window. I could see trees, plants, insects etc. all busy communicating. I saw my human self as just part of that same network, not superior, just part of the whole system. I laughed at the arrogance of us humans — who do we think we are? We just take over and don't realise we are destroying this precious network.

But why did I see it? I think because I had spent so much time in rest and meditation, and I became open to any possibility. I had surrendered way back when I was on the floor in the foetal position. I was completely open to whatever it took to be helped. The therapy had opened my mind and I had been questioning everything and that included how society becomes fixed in a certain way.

I think as we are growing up, we become more and more distracted by the human world. Very few of us get the opportunity to see what is going on beyond our limited view and this limited view becomes an illusion as we think that is all there is. We operate on the surface and rarely explore the depths.

I was given a chance to explore the depths, or rather, to explore deeper than I had ever done in my lifetime. There was no societal influence — it was me on my bed with my book beside me.

The breakdown was the catalyst, not only for a new way of being in the world, but for opening up to the unseen wonders of the universe.

But it wasn't just what I could see: I started communicating with everything! My psychic or sixth sense skills sharpened, and I seemed to be able to talk to everything! I would share these things with Jannelle and it was so nice that she didn't view me as crazy. I know most people would have thought I was off with the fairies – and in fact I really was!

I would talk from my bedroom to the tree outside and I would have 'people' visit. This never frightened me; it felt perfectly normal! One visit that has always stayed with me was a time when I was standing at the bathroom mirror brushing my hair, and out of the corner of my eye, I saw a hint of someone. When I tried to hang onto the image it was gone.

I learnt to relax and just let it flow. This person came again and again. He was an Aboriginal Elder in spirit – he told me he was from the Gumbaynggirr group, and I was living on their country.

He appeared with white hair and was carrying a spear. One day he brought me a shell necklace and placed it over my head. He never said much, and at times I found him quite severe. Then one day he started talking… and he was angry.

The talk was about the environment and his great sadness and anger that humans don't understand. **'The earth can live without you – you cannot live without the earth. You are destroying it – can't you hear it cry? You are a plague on its surface. You must stop now before it's too late.'** I would sit and nod in agreement.

> 'The earth can live without you – you cannot live without the earth. You are destroying it – can't you hear it cry?'

I asked him why he had come to me. He replied that I was one of the few people who had invited him in. But there was more. He said that he knew we (Doug and I) understood, and he wanted to talk. I replied that I didn't know much, but Doug certainly did. He disagreed and reminded me of the times I would sit in the bush on my own. He said, 'You appreciate the powers of the land.'

These sessions with him were both nerve-racking and amazing. He continued to visit for several years. I knew when he was around as I would have three incidents of dead animals, like a bird, snake or bandicoot, happen over three days. I would then sit down and wait for him to come.

He would often have messages for Doug about what he would like him to plant. In fact, he didn't want him to stop planting – and to this very day, Doug is planting trees!

It was hard for me to move from this world into our 'normal' world.

Once I was attending parent/ teacher interviews and I passed my friend Sheryl on the way out. I said to her, 'Sheryl, you know this is an illusion we live in.' She replied, 'I know!' We still have a laugh about it as it was such a bizarre thing to say as you pass someone you know at the school, but I knew I could tell Sheryl, for indeed she does know!

In fact, I shared the story with her of the Gumbaynggirr Elder visiting me. It gave me a deep respect for their ancient culture and I'm so happy that in these times they are getting the recognition they deserve – although there is still much work to be done.

Apart from living in a different world, I was seeing signs to help me along the way. I couldn't believe I hadn't seen the signs before, but of course I was still asleep. Now I had woken up I was looking forward to each day, wondering what exciting thing would happen!

It may have been something I would read in a book, a song I had heard, or something I saw in a movie or on TV – or something someone said to me. Here are some examples:

In the early days of my therapy, when I was still in the depths of depression, I fell asleep in front of the TV, watching a documentary on Sonny and Cher. As I woke again, I realised everyone had gone to bed. The TV was still on and the documentary was nearly finished, but as I sat up Sonny Bono suddenly seemed to be looking straight at me, smiling. He was saying, 'Dreams came true for me – it can happen to you too!'

'What?' I thought. 'Sonny Bono is in my loungeroom talking to me!' It was both bizarre and funny. At first, I doubted myself when these incidents happened, but over time I accepted that indeed they were happening.

When I was revisiting the teenage years, I had worked through the constant messages we received then from Mum: that magic didn't happen at our house and we were cursed with the Crawford's bad luck. I would then be out somewhere and parked next to me or driving in front of me would be cars with big 'Magic Happens' stickers on them.

The rational brain can say, well it's just coincidence, there are plenty of cars with those stickers on them, but in my state of heightened awareness, these signs were leaping out! There were so many ways that this happened.

Sometimes a shop assistant or receptionist would say something and it was like they were channelling the message I needed to hear for the day.

Many of my messages came from songs, and some of these I'd like to share. I am a Beatles fan, so I often played their music and at this time of my life I was hearing their songs like I had never heard them before. How often had I heard Paul McCartney's song *'Blackbird'* – but at that time it was like I REALLY heard it.

But the song that stood out for me and that I have carried ever since is George Harrison's *'Within You Without You.'*

In all the years I'd had the Sgt. Peppers album, I'd never truly listened to this. Suddenly it stopped me in my tracks. He'd seen what I'd discovered! He'd felt the white light, he'd seen beyond the illusion, he'd seen the connection! 'Oh my God!' I said to myself. 'He knew THEN! Way back then!'

I rushed to my book to write to God about it...

He knew!!!

Of course he knew! Many people know!

But... why don't more people see it then?

Heather, The Beatles were the messengers, and there are many messengers. There are messages every day! But only some humans see it. To see it requires your defences to be let down – it requires time and stillness – something which seems to be in short supply. It is why people have these awakenings during a crisis like yours. You will find many writings on the connected world if you go searching, but very few humans see it. But that's okay! Enjoy what

you have seen, treasure it. And when more people understand, you will all benefit. Humans are the link that causes most grief in the world, we do hope that they can eventually advance.

So... are you saying humans are slow learners? Are we all dumb?

No! But many are very self-absorbed. When they can really feel they are a link, like every other living thing, life will be better for them and for everything else.

I'd like to help. How can I help?

You don't need to think about how you can help – it will just happen.

God, can you tell me what I'm talking to? In Sunday School, their God seemed to be a man in the clouds!

Look at the song. I am within you and without you. You've felt that!

So – you are love.

Yes.

All you need is love.

Yes.

Great song by the Beatles.

It certainly is!

I would sit and smile when I had these revelations. I felt like I had access to a secret treasure chest, like I had been let into the biggest secret that is kept from the human population. It gave me such confidence and, when I could stay in that space, the fear melted away. In its place was pure joy!

But I was still searching. What was I searching for? I had found love; I'd found the real world behind the illusion — what more could I want?

The answer to that was contained in the writings to my child self.

MY LEARNINGS

- Through my quiet times and reflection, I discovered a hidden world which is so much fun!

- I learnt that messages are everywhere – we just have to truly see them.

- I saw how small humans are in the context of the universal web of connection.

- I had several 'visitors,' but the Aboriginal Elder was the most consistent and shared an important message about the environment.

FOR THE READER

🦋 Through meditation and quiet, you can access much of what is unseen in the normal world. When you spend time in this space, your worries melt away. You are just left in a place of pure enjoyment and you are never alone!

Chapter Eleven

It Was Always About The Horses

'Let yourself be silently drawn by the strange pull of what you really love. It will not lead you astray.'

— **Rumi**

When I started on this journey, the only goal I had was to remove the depression and anxiety that had been plaguing me throughout my life. I didn't want to end up crying in the corner again. I just wanted to be happy and carefree.

I had no idea then that the therapy would stir up buried desires and long forgotten memories. As time went on, and I started to recover parts of myself, I knew I was on the wrong track with my university course. Now I didn't want to become a counsellor! I realised I had chosen that field as it was the only way I could feel that I belonged. I had always been a good listener and I know I was a good counsellor in my days of Nursing Mothers.

I was good at the jobs I did – but I wasn't PASSIONATE about them! **Through the conversations with my child self,**

> Through the conversations with my child self, I had discovered my true passion...

I had discovered my true passion which had been buried years ago, but it was overwhelming, and I needed to be sure.

I turned to meditation, during which I would ask what I was meant to do, but the answer was vague. I would be told to enjoy myself and I had no idea what that meant. Then one day during meditation I found a very kind man standing in front of me and he told me I was ready to hear what I was truly passionate about. My younger self appeared, and she was about nine years old. She was sitting on a rock smiling. She said to me:

> YH: You know! You've loved it all your life! You rode to the kind ladies as a pre-schooler, and you were fascinated by cowboy movies. The first thing you asked when you knew you were moving to the country was if you could learn to ride! You've loved horses ALL your life!
>
> Why did you cry when you read that story about Tex? Why did you cry when you remembered the kind lady at the riding school? Why did you have the courage to approach the principal about the riding lessons? Why did you feel 'dead' in the city? Why do you feel so great at the horse place? Why

is that the only thing you wanted to do when you had your anxiety attacks? And why did you cry when you saw the sign at Valery Trails, hanging in the tree... 'It is here in the spirit of the wind that I will find my soul.' You went and read that sign week after week!

But you've been too scared to embrace it. You don't think you know enough – but you're learning. But more than that – there is so much you already know. You don't think you do but you do.

The horses need us!'

AH: 'The horses need us? What for?' I said.

She told me to go and check all I had written – and by then I had filled about five A4 lecture notebooks! I went through all my notes: the facts about my life, my writings to my child self and my writings to God.

First, I looked at all my conversations with my child self, from the beginning:

I wanted to fly on my magic horse to the Kingdom of the Kind Ladies – I cried because I wanted to live there forever with them and the horses.

I wanted to learn to ride when I knew we were moving to the country. It's the first thing I asked to do.

I would regularly talk to my young self when I came home from my weekly trail rides. I would ask her how she felt about the horses:

> YH: I think they are magical. I feel wonderful on them. It's like they're from a fairy tale, it's something about their warmth. I don't know if I'm meant to do more. It's like owning a horse has always been denied to me. I used to envy those horse girls.

When I was trying to confirm the feelings, I would ask her to talk about it. She would say, 'When I'm with them I feel like I've come home.'

These words stood out: I FEEL LIKE I'VE COME HOME. This was obviously a huge part of who I was.

This conversation was from when I was working on regrets about my career choice.

> **AH: Let's play the 'what if' game. Before you left school, if all possibilities had been there, if your mum was encouraging you to look at all of them – picture it – art and design courses, horse courses, travel courses, swimming coach. They are all laid out and your mum is saying, 'Heather, this is all great. You can have a really good career and I'll help you find out more. Make sure you do what you love.' What are you picking?**

> YH: Oh! It would have been so exciting! I would have examined all of them. But in the end, I would have picked the horses – without a doubt.

And in the conversation above, the last words – WITHOUT A DOUBT – stood out. At the time I was having these discussions, I would look at what I had written and then move on. It was almost too scary looking at it!

•●•

In the middle of this exploration of the buried horse passion, I started to buy horse magazines. I couldn't believe what was in one that I bought. There was a story about the history of the Tamworth Pony Club and Tex's involvement with the club.

He taught me to ride. I loved those afternoons! He was a shining light in those dark years. It's such a coincidence that I picked up this magazine and found out all about him. He had died six years previously.

Once again, I started sobbing. It was like he had come back from the dead to reach out and help me – to help that little girl remove the barriers. I remembered that in those days, after we dropped the horses off at their paddock, he would double me back to their house on his horse and always say, 'Don't worry! I've got you!'

And he did have me. He was there – helping me to let go of my fears. The very thing I loved to do, and I had felt like I wasn't allowed to really be part of it. Now it was my time.

•●•

If this longing was correct, I knew it would mean a whole lifestyle change. It would mean embracing the horse journey fully.

I played 'The Deathbed Game.' If I was on my deathbed, what regrets would I have? The answer was that I would regret never owning a horse. And it was the only regret. Wow!

I was still caught between two worlds and becoming more and more exhausted, yet I was never too tired to go on my weekly trail ride. It was energising, yet the battle between

> I played 'The Deathbed Game.' If I was on my deathbed, what regrets would I have?

Conservative Heather and Real Heather was all consuming and exhausting.

I was constantly fighting my new urges because it seemed out of character. Instead, I was just tired, and I had no urge to do anything around the house. I had another conversation. I still addressed it to my young self, but I was in fact talking to my true self.

> **AH: What's going on? What are you battling against?**

> YH: I'm struggling to be a conservative person – to be doing chores around the house. I think everyone is shocked about my constant riding. When I told Mum about it, she said, 'Oh you aren't going to become one of those dreadful horse people who live in a mess!' She was joking but it touched something. I felt myself bristling.

> **AH: You're sick of being the 'Present Heather.' The real one is underneath trying to get out and sometimes she's tired because it's hard. Other times new and old Heather merge for a while and you have lots of energy.**

I started crying after I wrote that – I had worked out that there was quite a battle going on, and my real self was fighting desperately to lose the outer false shell. I asked my young self what sort of person Real Heather is.

> YH: She's a person who is a bit eccentric. She doesn't care too much about clothes or possessions. She likes to live in a place with a nice feel to it. She

loves the country around her – she loves to watch the wind and the trees. She loves earthy things and also nice people… and she just loves those horses! She can't believe she forgot that!! It's such a passion!

AH: So why do you get tired?

YH: When I can't see an opening – I'm suffocating. It's easier to be tired when I live in fear. Mum said to me it's like I've just given up. She's been worried about me because I haven't had any interest in anything – but I still don't have those interests back. It's like I'm just creating new ones, so she worries that I'm having my second childhood, midlife crisis, menopause etc.

AH: And what are you having?

YH: A battle between my soul and my wounded child – Real Heather vs Conservative Heather.

AH: Who's winning?

YH: Real Heather.

It wasn't easy. I was going through a metamorphosis and there was quite a struggle. Part of me wanted to embrace the horse passion fully, the other part was hoping it would wear off, that I would just 'get better' and go back on my familiar but impossible path.

It was the written conversations I had with God that really brought it all out and moved me beyond the battle.

God, I'm in tears tonight – over horses! I'm sad it all ended. I loved it when I was young. I could get a horse now, but I'm scared. I don't know why I'm so emotional. I've even looked at my old horse books from when I was young. I know the pictures so well. I feel sad for the little girl in me. I'm so confused!

Yes, you do love horses. It was certainly a passion with you. But your parents weren't in a position to help you much. They knew you loved it, and your Mum did what she could with the lessons.

I forgot... I can't believe I forgot!

Yes – you forgot how much you loved it. And you're right, you're good at it. Yes, you could have gone far – and don't think you can't! But... maybe in a different way to what you expect!

What do you mean?

Let's just say it will all present itself when it should.

But I have no confidence. I'm scared. How can I get confidence?

It may surprise you that you know way more about horses than you think!

Oh! I know nothing! Well, what should I do?

Nothing! You've acknowledged your feelings so let it flow!

• ● •

God, I cry now when I hear about animals who have a relationship with their owners.

What is it about the animals?

It's about the horses mainly – I think I could be good with them. I don't mean riding them. I could be good around them. Maybe they're my extended family.

You're crying...

It's the connection – they help people. I must help them – it's something about that. I must help them! But how? I don't know how!

That horse you rode – you asked if it had been mistreated. It made you feel emotional.

Yes. It's like, I feel so sorry for them. They're so nervous, I just like to treat them gently. I almost feel like they're my children. I want to look after them.

Well, I will tell you this – you know more than you think you do.

• ● •

These conversations shocked and surprised me. I had only ever been on the outskirts of the horse world as a child. I went for riding lessons and now I was going on trail rides — but I wasn't a horse person like some people who grow up around them and live and breathe them.

But I was starting to realise that perhaps I WAS a horse person, but I had ended up on a different path — and now my path had become almost impossible for me to walk on. To cross to a new path would require a huge leap of faith — but what did I have to lose?

Why did I have such a fear of owning a horse? Was it just the commitment or expense? Or was it more? I knew a horse wasn't going to solve all my problems — in fact, it would probably create more problems. I also knew that our land, while being able to maintain a horse, wasn't really the best place for horse ownership.

It wasn't really that either. As an 11-year-old I had watched other kids go to Pony Club. I remember visiting my friend at one camp. She wasn't even really horse mad, but a relative had a horse and she went to the week-long camp. I just felt 'lesser' and left out. In my young mind I had already seen myself as different to them, particularly after my father's death. This was reinforced when we moved back to the city. I had wonderful moments of being able to ride, but it was really just an aside.

As I moved into the workforce, I had the occasional ride, particularly when moving back to the country, but then my attention was turned to friends, marriage, then children. Combined with this were the many moves we had in a short period of time. I had not been around horses for over 25 years, and now it was consuming my every thought.

The barrier was pure fear. I knew it was a lifestyle and mindset change and I was scared. It was off the safe path that Mum had encouraged me to stay on. What was I going to do?

I had to remember that there was nothing to fear.

MY LEARNINGS

- My breakdown wasn't just about my wounded self; it was because I had reached a dead end on the path I was travelling.

- My child self knew all along what my real passion was.

- I learnt how easily we can find our true path – and how easily we can brush it aside.

- The only barrier to my passion was fear.

FOR THE READER

- When we get to mid-life, we often search for meaning in our lives. In fact I could write a whole book about it – and maybe I will! There are many ways you can explore this, but the first way is to find stillness. Find a time each day when you can relax and enjoy a short meditation.

- Start writing – it doesn't have to be to your child self, it can be to anyone! It can just be your thoughts. The act of getting them down on paper lets you sort through what is truly important to you.

- Play 'The Deathbed Game' – it may surprise you to see what arises.

Chapter Twelve

Following The Dream

'We both crave and fear truly becoming ourselves.'

— Abraham Maslow

I edged closer and closer to getting a horse. At the time, Emma was also fully absorbed in the horse world. She was still going to Valery Trails on the weekend, but she really wanted to go to Pony Club.

Maybe this was the opening I needed. Somehow it seemed easier to get a horse for her, rather than myself. My riding friends were encouraging me also, so I started looking. I found there was a place nearby selling some of their trail horses and they had one horse left. In fact, our Adventure Girls group had been riding there and my friend Sheryl had ridden Quill, the horse for sale! I arranged a time for Emma and I to go and look at him. Emma fell in love with him immediately. He was a Clydesdale cross – a very big horse for a little girl – but there she was hugging him!

Was I really going to buy a horse? I was so scared. We went home to think about it and arranged to visit a second time the following weekend. On the drive there I was thinking about how easy it was when I was a child to think about owning a horse. I had no idea what was involved! I thought a horse could just live in our backyard! As an adult, I knew what it would entail. Even though we had paddocks, I knew there would be feed costs, horse equipment costs, hoof trimming, vet costs and daily care. My brain was busy with the practicalities, when a song came on the radio: 'Beautiful Day' by U2. I knew it was being played for me.

The words that had meaning for me were in the chorus: I mustn't let it get away! Okay – I took note!

Again, Emma and Quill seemed to get on so well and I also had a ride on him. He did seem like a nice horse, so what was I going to do? We went into the owner's house to talk about it. They'd had five horses for sale and the others had already been sold. There were several other people enquiring about Quill, so I needed to decide. Emma of course was looking at me, begging for me to say yes. I knew that the contract to buy was pending a vet check and would also include a 14-day trial. Surely it would be okay.

I heard myself saying, 'Okay, we will take him.' Was that really my voice? Was I really buying a horse? In that moment the same song played on the radio in their house – 'Beautiful Day.' I knew then that it was indeed. I was really buying a horse. I had waited 44 years for this day, and indeed it WAS a beautiful day!

It was November 2000 – a year since my breakdown – and now I was to become a horse owner! What a year! **I never dreamt that the longing for a horse had been buried deep within me. I was so thankful for my breakdown as**

it had truly been a gift. Owning Quill was to become the catalyst for change in so many ways.

I arranged for Quill to go to my friend Cathy's property as our paddocks were occupied by horses on agistment. We had agreed to that when I thought no horse would be coming to our property. It was much better at our friend's place as Emma could ride with Cathy's daughter. We spent many days there and Quill proved to be a very good horse.

Meanwhile, Doug was feeling like everything had converged on him. Having Quill in the family added more pressure to him and changed the family dynamic. Emma and I were so often south of town with Quill. At the time I wondered why it would worry him as we were still in the depths of our troubles. But it did.

We eventually moved Quill back to our house when the people moved the horses off our land and put them in the paddock next door. Doug spent quite some time fencing in preparation. It was much easier with Quill at home. I sometimes rode him up the hill nearby, and I also used him as part of a TAFE course I did on horse care which included riding.

> I was so thankful for my breakdown as it had truly been a gift.

Emma started riding with the Bellingen Pony Club and soon became known as the little girl with the giant horse! She loved those days, and I was so happy to see her doing what I would have loved to do.

I learnt more from owning Quill than I ever did on the horse care course. I learnt about sweet itch, stone bruises, various lotions and potions, saddles, fly masks and rugs! I also learnt about injuries!

Quill cut himself badly on a fence, then he had some soreness. I learnt about horse chiropractors and acupuncture and various vets – and I also learnt that 13-year-old girls can lose interest and want to go shopping and to the movies with friends!

I knew this might happen, and Emma, to her credit, did what she could for Quill, but I could see she just didn't have the passion I did. Like almost 90 percent of horse-mad girls, the phase wore off. It's only a few who carry that passion on.

It was difficult caring for him – not because of the actual care, but the way our house and property was set out was all so very awkward.

It was built off the side of a hill and in winter, the sun disappeared by midday and in summer you were blasted by the sun from the minute you woke up. But it was the separation from the land that made it hard – it didn't have easy connection to the paddocks.

I knew that we needed to move. But I was so scared. I had many conversations with my friend God. Here is one:

God, Do I really move from here? It's like a dream spot!

Is it? Who says?

Well, it's near the ocean, close to town...

Is that your dream?

I thought it was... I'm so unsettled! I see some places that look great, but then I think of the kids getting to school and how far they are from town.

Heather, what do you REALLY want?

I want a farm! But I don't want to be too far from town.

Heather – this time –

GO WITH YOUR HEART – not your head. Forget the 'list.' If you love the feel, it's the right one. Everything else will fall into place. YOU MUST BE COMFORTABLE AND REALLY FEEL AT HOME. Choose love, not fear. Really choose love! The practicalities will fall into place. If you are meant to be there, things will conspire to make that happen. I'm with you Heather – through it all.

But will I be happy anywhere?

Heather, you know true happiness comes from within. But you are not happy where you live and finding a place you love will help.

I convinced Doug that we needed to find more land. He didn't really want to move as he had all his plants set up and his newly-created gardens were growing, but the thought of more land appealed to him.

We decided we would look north and south of Coffs Harbour, with a limit of 20 minutes into town. The kids still had to get to their school for a few more years, but I wanted to find something that would suit us long after they had flown the nest.

It was the middle of 2001 and so much had happened in 18 months. I never dreamt several years earlier that we would be searching for more land. In fact, I thought we would be looking for something smaller!

We spent a weekend driving south of town. I had marked some places that were for sale, and I wanted to see what they looked like, but nothing jumped out at me.

The following weekend we headed north. There was land advertised and I thought it would be worth looking at. There were two blocks of 100 acres next to each other and they were being subdivided from a much larger grazing property. The problem was, there was no road access, no power, two small gullies to cross and the cleared part of the block was a sea of Setaria grass – standing as tall as us.

That didn't stop me exploring this land! I sent Doug out in front to disturb any snakes and to clear any spider webs. He helped me through the gullies and pushed through the long grass, while I followed in the newly-made track.

As I walked further up the hill there were patches where the grass wasn't so long. I said to Doug, 'This is feeling good!' He agreed. We made it to the top of the hill and flattened some of the grass. The view was outstanding! We could see the distant hills, forests and farmland, yet we felt so private.

I fell in love – right there on top of the hill. To the north was a mountain range, to the west were distant hills, to the south were more hills, forest and farmland, and to the east was forest. This was it! We were more excited than we had been in a long time, and it was wonderful for both of us to be excited. But before we got carried away, we needed details; for instance, we had no idea where the boundaries were.

We wasted no time in ringing the agent and were able to get a map. Now we could see clearly the two blocks for sale. The map had grid references and Doug could use his GPS system to find those exact points. The land consisted of about 60 acres of forest on the eastern side and the rest was open land with a small creek running through it. The western side was bound by a larger creek which ran through the valley.

We were over the moon! It was perfect! It was 20 minutes from town and had all the features we were looking for. These blocks had been on the market for 18 months as they were considered too expensive. There was no power, water or road. You were starting from scratch.

After some negotiation, we agreed on a price. We had stretched ourselves to our limits financially – in fact, Doug thought it was the riskiest financial move he had ever made! However, we then found out it would cost us a small fortune to have the power connected as it required a new transformer. On top of this, another couple were interested in the property… I was in tears. We would have to pull out. We just couldn't afford the costs for the power.

I told Doug to ring the agent and let him know we were out of the running. When he rang, the agent said to him, 'Don't worry about that. I've convinced this couple the other block is very worthwhile and with the two of you purchasing, the power company now provides the transformer for free.'

I felt like I had won the lottery! It was still ours! We paid our deposit and each weekend we would visit it as it was only ten minutes from our house. The owner burnt all the long grass, and while it was full of charcoal for a while, we were able to see the cleared area in more detail.

The creek flats were a good size and the climb to the top of the hill was relatively gentle. Standing in the middle of the large creek flat was a single tree. When I saw it, I started shaking my head and sobbing. It was the tree from my meditation – I had found my baby self under this tree! And now here it was! It looked magical. The tree from my dreams! It is now named The Magic Tree.

I had really come home! I could feel it! The land felt comforting — like it just enveloped you. I felt very secure and protected. It was like I was in a dreamland paradise.

•●•

We had paid a deposit, but contracts weren't exchanged until the end of December 2001, and settlement would not be until April 2002. During this time there was a serious threat to our land.

A highway bypass route was being proposed for Coffs Harbour. An alternative route running through the middle of our 60 acres of forest was on the cards. Our eastern boundary backed onto a forest road that ran along the ridge. You could walk through our forest and across this road and look beyond to the ocean. All this beautiful, forested area would be affected.

We were devastated. We stared in disbelief at the map with the proposed route. I felt physically ill, not just for the loss of our dream property, but for the proposed destruction. The area in question would take out so much forest.

I was also heartbroken. This land had been calling us and every obstacle to ownership had fallen away, but now there was an obstacle that would be too great to overcome. I tried to think rationally. We had not exchanged contracts so we would only lose a small amount and we could look elsewhere. What was the big deal?

I knew what it was. Of all the places I had lived in my life, I had never felt like this. It was a special feeling. I knew we truly belonged on this patch of land. This was my homecoming – not just my physical homecoming, my spiritual homecoming. THIS was the place. It had our name on it way before we even knew it existed…

Again, I turned to my God book.

> *God, you say don't choose fear, choose love, but it's a pretty big thing to buy a block AND be threatened by a highway!*
>
> **Heather, all this may not happen. It may not affect you. You don't know what the future holds.**
>
> *No, I don't! That's why it's so hard.*
>
> **Heather don't be put off by fear, especially if you love it. You've talked about all its features, you've wavered between being practical and being impulsive. FEEL IT! Really feel it!**
>
> *I do have to get away from here, but that doesn't mean that the land is right.*
>
> **What was your first feeling on it?**
>
> *I liked it – it felt right, then when all this happened, I got scared. But my real feeling is to take it and enjoy it. Then again, I rushed into this house and it was all wrong!*
>
> **No – it was right. It was perfectly right for you to be in this house, but now you know it's time to move.**

But what if it happens?

If it does it will all work out. This is what helps you grow. There will always be challenges and decisions in life! But I'm with you – there is nothing to fear!

We agonised over whether to pull out before the contracts were exchanged and I did much writing in my book. It was those writings that helped me to keep faith. I had to choose love. We both loved the land – we loved it with a passion – and didn't want to give it up. Doug even decided that he would follow any messages I got from my writing, or any other signs I saw.

Once we decided to go ahead and exchange contracts, Doug joined the group protesting the highway bypass through that particular route. People were fighting to save their valley and to save the rare patch of rainforest that it would run through. I hoped my Aboriginal guide could in some way influence the decision.

In March 2002 we heard that the route had been taken off the table. It would be built where it was originally planned – around the western outskirts of Coffs Harbour. We had taken a leap of faith, and now it was such good news! We were elated! The stress of a possible highway had taken a huge toll on us. In fact, the past two years had taken a toll – our marriage had been in turmoil and now we were moving again.

But a few months later we found that the council was investigating that route again to present the case for it to the state government. By that time, we were the owners.

My writings to God continued. The answer I always got was, 'Your land is safe.' I had to hope that was right and to keep on planning for a house. During this time, we were madly making improvements to our other house in preparation for sale.

• ● •

While Quill was the catalyst for me to move from the house I disliked so much, sadly, I ended up selling him. I agonised over the decision, but it came to a head as his seasonal itch got worse and the horses from the paddock next door were taken away. Now he was all alone, and he was sad. Emma was no longer going to Pony Club and it would take a year or two to get set up at our new property.

Before we sold Quill, I took him to my friend's place, where he stayed for a month or so. I would go down and ride him, and it was on Quill that I had the best trail ride I've ever had. Quill never felt like my horse though – he was Emma's horse – and now he needed to be with someone else and in a climate that was more suitable. I knew that my next step was to prepare the house for sale, something which took two years!

Late one evening, the transport truck turned up. Emma and I sobbed as Quill was led away. He was going south, and we were sent photos of him enjoying his new life. I was relieved as he was surrounded by kids and other horses.

I have so much to thank him for. He was my first experience of horse ownership and the reason we went searching for a better place. If it wasn't for him, I would not have found our land which I named Homecoming Farm.

So much had happened – I had owned a horse – and now we were going to be moving to a new home, but there was something else that happened during this time. I experienced a grief that was so deep, I didn't even know it was there – until I did.

Get yourself a coffee or something stronger, then settle in and read about my revelation!

MY LEARNINGS

- I took the leap of faith and bought a horse. I learnt that you can make your dreams a possibility, but it won't be without hard work and lots of learning!

- If you always listen to other people, you will never hear yourself. In the case of the house move, other people thought we were mad to move from our property to start from scratch on our land. I didn't listen to them!

- I learnt to choose the feel of a place, rather than what it had or didn't have.

FOR THE READER

🦋 Sometimes, you have to let go of fear and take a leap of faith for your own mental wellbeing. It may or may not work out – but it's better than spending your life on the edge of the cliff. You will find that most of the time, it does work out!

Chapter Thirteen

The Remembering

'The mind, once stretched by a new idea, never returns to its original dimensions.'

— Ralph Waldo Emerson

'There are reasons for everything, and no coincidences exist on the path of destiny.'

— Brian L. Weiss

November 2000 was a significant month. Not only did we buy Quill, but I also discovered something else.

Throughout this time I was still having my sessions with Jannelle. She had been through every step of the way with me, and I will be forever grateful. I was almost standing on my own two feet again, with a new me in place. I had remembered what I was passionate about and had followed through on this passion by buying a horse, and now I was thinking that we really did need to move to another property.

My thoughts were much happier, and I was functioning so much better with day-to-day life. Doug and I were resolving our differences, and life was much brighter.

I had spent a year examining my whole life in detail and now I was forging ahead on a new path. There was nothing more to be revealed – or so I thought.

•●•

On Remembrance Day, 2000 we were watching the movie *Gallipoli*, the brilliant but sad WWI drama film directed by Peter Weir. It's an incredibly sad movie and I was in tears at the end which is quite normal, but instead of recovering I became more distressed to the point where I went into the bedroom and sat in the corner crying.

Doug walked in and said, 'I know it was a sad movie, but it wasn't THAT sad!'

I replied, 'Don't you get it? I was there!'

What did I just say? I was in the war? We were both stunned by my words.

'Well, I wasn't *right* there but I was there! In the war! Oh! Such good mates! Some of them didn't come home. I can smell the leather, the saddles, the horses. Oh! How could I shoot my horse! I shot my horse!'

But it was the emotion coming up. I thought my heart would break. My whole body shook as I cried, and my skin was damp with sweat. In fact, I was no longer crying, I was howling! Where was this coming from?

Eventually the crying returned to sobs – and from deep in my memory I knew.

I was seeing my grandfather's life in the war. I sat there shaking. After my year of therapy, I thought I'd done the hard yards. Now what was happening?

Doug had learnt to go along with these things. He was often thankful it didn't involve him – that he hadn't been the cause of my latest round of tears. However, by that time my tears had been much more infrequent. I was almost 'normal' again.

Now the tears were flowing! The following morning it was no different. I had managed to sleep but now the same feeling was there, and it was mainly feelings of deep grief – about shooting my horse.

I could only assume it was one of two things: genetic memory or, in fact, I had been my grandfather. We all have our own views on this, and I don't have a conclusive answer – none of us do! I had not been a believer in past life experiences. I had felt it was very 'New Age' and gimmicky – but to FEEL it was a different story! And I was feeling it. Boy, was I feeling it!

For me, it felt like a past life experience and it continued, but it was the grief I felt that I could not hold back that was so significant.

I rang Jannelle and, through my sobs, I told her the story. She replied, 'Well – that makes perfect sense to me, as you tell me. You have grieved so much of all the things that have happened to you and now you're deeply grieving your grandfather's experience and living it as your very own. And now you know something else about why this horse theme is so important to you.'

I said 'So, I haven't gone mad?'

'Not at all' she replied.

I also did some writing as it seemed too unbelievable. I had to get confirmation from a source I trusted – and I trusted Jannelle and my best friend God:

> **God, I want to talk about that movie Gallipoli. I cried so hard after that – for all those men. I felt it. I really felt it! The grief, the wasted lives. They were crying for their mums. It was like I was there – I could smell the leather, the gunfire, everything! Like I was part of it, and I ended up in the corner of the bedroom again, sobbing. Was I in the Light Horse?**
>
> **Yes.**
>
> **Is that why I cried?**
>
> **Yes.**
>
> **Was I my grandfather?**
>
> **Yes.**

Is that the attraction to a farm – and my love of horses?

Yes.

God – this is too weird! Just let me comprehend this! Oh! I'm all shivery...

But you've always known... you've just forgotten. That's the attachment.

I can't believe this! I'm so emotional!

I had to drive into town the next day. We were at the stage with the kids where I ran 'Mum's Taxi', so these trips were frequent. I happened to have a CD playing in the car – Dragon's Greatest Hits. Dragon was a famous band in the 70s, from New Zealand originally and then based in Australia.

A song came on, called *'On The Beach Head'* and again something touched me. It was like my grandfather was talking directly to me. I cannot quote the lyrics here, but he was saying – well you've got quite a story, what are you going to do about it?

I certainly did have a tale to tell. What was I going to do with it? Was he talking to me? Was he expecting me to do something? I didn't know – I was just still so shocked by the revelation.

I asked Mum if she knew much about Dad's father. She said he had died before they met but she had heard the stories of how he had to shoot his horse and how much he loved him. I started to cry, but pretended I needed to do something else so I could compose myself. I didn't want Mum to know about this.

I needed to ask God about the horse.

God, I'm searching for THAT horse, aren't I?

Yes.

But will I find him?

You will.

Why is there so much emotion?

The war had a huge impact on your life. It WAS your life! You're just remembering.

I just can't believe the tears – they won't stop. If people knew they would think I'm crazy!

You know you're not. You're just remembering – stepping from one life to another. You never got over shooting him: you lost a part of yourself. But it's okay. He knew your love. They all know – the horses...

They all know?.... All the horses know?

Yes, it will become clearer to you as time goes on. Don't worry about it now – just know that they know your love.

As the weeks went on, my tears were never far away. I told some friends who I knew would understand, but I could never tell them the part about shooting the horse without crying. I was having visions regularly of the horse's eye – always the same vision – the eye staring at me. I imagined that was what I saw just before I shot it.

Once again, I wrote to my best friend.

God, this horse, my grandad's horse – he never got over it. It was like shooting a child. A part of him died. He grieved for that horse. That's what killed him.

Yes – he did.

So why am I so emotional?

The grief was held in for so long, so just finish the grieving. You lost that horse in the worst possible way, but it was meant to be. The horse knew that and knew he was loved – it's okay to grieve.

Did he really know he was loved?

Yes, he knew he was special, he knew his work was done. But just like grieving for your dad, take time.

•●•

And the grieving took so much time! Again, I've written, and this was several months after my first awareness.

The agony! I killed my horse – I loved him! I loved that life, even though it was war.

Write with your other hand – you need to get this out.

His eye! I can see his eye! I loved him like a child. I loved being with him! I loved the leather, the saddle. I served a purpose. I could have done it all my life. After the war, no one understood. They didn't understand about the horses. I loved them.

The Remembering

What didn't they understand?

They just didn't understand the bond, the connection. I never forgot him. I loved him more than anything.

What about your family?

I loved my family, but they didn't understand.

Why did you die?

I didn't want to live any longer. I wanted to go to him.

And again I have written…

God, I'm upset about the war again. I thought I was over it.

Write with your other hand…

It was scary. My horse was my friend. I was safe in the saddle.

What upsets you so much?

The sadness. We were something. My horse.

Why is it coming up now?

Because of the horses.

It's truly what you're here to do isn't it. And to find your horse.

Yes, I never resolved it.

And this is your chance. So, your tears are the remembering.

And people are honouring us and the horses.

You wanted that sort of adventure again.

Yes.

What is it all about – is it a message – or just a remembering?

Everything – and I'm close to finding him.

Yes – you are.

And again, another month goes by. I had already decided I wanted my own horse, but now I found myself searching for this particular horse as I knew he was out there.

God, Grandfather is still causing me grief. It's just haunting me: the war, the horse, the mates. He really died in 1919. He just existed after. I need to live – not exist.

Well, you're on your way to it. You need to find your horse.

I might go to the horse sale. But I'm so fussy!

Well, you're not just after any horse! But let the other one go – grieve him and your exciting life – but when you are finished, life will be exciting again. Don't be in mourning for two lifetimes!

I didn't realise I was until recently!

I know. See how much it all fits? See why horses are such a big part of your life? Your love for them is very deep-seated. It goes back even further but we won't go there now! You've always known it Heather – always – that little girl knew.

I realise that now.

Five months later I was STILL talking about it!

God, that horse saved my life, didn't it?

Yes.

I never got over that. I had to take its life. I loved it. That horse meant more to me than anything. If not for him, I would have been dead in the war. I'm forever grateful – I just want to help it. Where is it? I owe it. I owe all of them! I lived and breathed them. I knew them so well. They were our faithful companions.

Yes Heather – that's been hard for you to live with. That's your grief.

But I need to resolve it. I don't know how!

MAGIC HAPPENS

So you say – but when?

When the universe is ready.

I just want a chance to repay this horse and to repay all the horses. I'm searching the horse sales. Where else should I look?

Heather – it will happen when you least expect it. I know it's hard living with this grief, but you need to embrace it to know what it is. Don't see the grief as bad – even if it's hard to let go. Love is so special in all forms. Treasure it.

Remember – WHEN YOU LEAST EXPECT IT – your horse will appear.

I continued these conversations regularly, and there were still songs and other messages that touched me. One of these was the song *'Time Immemorial'* by Crowded House. It felt like my grandfather was singing it to me.

I asked God.

Why does this song make me cry? I understand that we will always be trying to find the invincible one. Is the invincible one you God?

It's YOU Heather – YOU!

For time immemorial you will try to find yourself – your real self – and you will try to remember who you are! That's what you are hearing in that song. Even if the writers have a different meaning to their songs, you are hearing what you need to hear!

So, I'm being reminded all the time that I AM powerful.

Indeed, you are! And you need to be reminded. The habit of fear is very strong. Without fear, what would you do – now that you have found your land?

Well, with the horses, I'd like to teach them with kindness, and I'd like to have gatherings with horses and people. But sometimes I feel I'm too old and I don't really know anything. I'm a beginner!

If you know what you'd like to do, it doesn't matter if it takes you the rest of your life! Don't worry! Everything will fall into place. There is never a grand finale. One thing may lead to another – the stepping stones of life – but just keep on picking the right track.

I kept searching for this horse that I had shot. I went to horse sales, looked in magazines… and I would keep asking God where the horse was. I would get the same answer:

> WHEN YOU LEAST EXPECT IT,
> YOUR HORSE WILL APPEAR.

•●•

I had the past life revelation in November 2000, and it was now May 2002. We were the owners of Homecoming Farm and made regular trips out there to plan and just take it all in. I resigned myself to focus on the move and prepare the house for sale. Quill had been sold and I certainly didn't need another horse at that time.

One morning I was having my shower, busy thinking about plans for the day ahead. The vision of the horse's eye appeared in front of me as it had on so many other occasions. I was a little surprised as I had been focused on the sale of the house for once, not the horse!

I was staring at the image when something different happened – another eye appeared. There is a moment in time, a split second, when you go from confusion to realisation. The second eye was Doug's eye – his eye moved across over the horse's eye and they melded together.

I fell to the floor in shock – water still running – and sobbed. He was the horse! I had been looking for a horse, but the horse had been with me for the last 20 years!

HE WAS THE HORSE!

God was right! When I least expected it, the horse appeared! I managed to get out of the shower and compose myself. It was the busy time of the morning – getting kids organised for school and making the dash to the school bus. Doug was away for work, so I had some space to take in this revelation.

I dropped the kids off, and rushed back into the house, jumped on my bed, and threw open my God book.

God! Can people have been other animals in past lives?

Hmmm, well let's see... why not?

God – you're being a bit flippant!

Heather, expand your mind! Of course! Never think narrow!

Well then – Doug is my horse.

Correct – she's got it!

It all makes sense! I used him for my power. He's been pushing me out on my own!

When you reclaim your power, as you have been, he won't push you out.

So, I've been searching for this horse at the sales and he's right here!

Don't worry, you will find a horse. But you won't need it – it will need you!

That's what the eyes were about – I loved his eyes. It was his eyes I was first attracted to, and I couldn't get the horse's eye out of my head. He's steady and reliable, like the horse, but I've needed him to save me.

You are going through the process of standing on your own two feet now you're aware. You'll be able to move on and will grow in confidence now you're on the right track.

I will look at Doug differently now!

He's very connected to the earth – that's no accident.

I kept this to myself until Doug returned the following weekend. When we were driving out to our land, I said to Doug, 'I'm going to tell you something and you have to promise not to laugh!' He looked puzzled.

'I've found the horse I was searching for, the one that Grandfather had to shoot.'

'Oh no! We're not ready for another horse!' he replied.

'You don't have to worry about that.'

'Why don't I? What are you going to do with it until we move?' he replied. He looked exasperated – he couldn't believe I had another horse when I had decided to wait until we were set up.

'Just listen to me! The horse is you! You were the horse I shot... I shot you!' I sobbed.

Now, I waited for him to start laughing, but he didn't. He was taking it in.

He said, 'Okay – I can accept that – in a way it makes sense.'

I replied, 'I know it's a bit out there – but it came to me this week.'

He nodded.

We then drove in silence and I knew he was processing that. I smiled to myself and said, 'It's been almost 100 years. We've been waiting for land and now we're coming home, together.'

We drove along the makeshift road up the hill to our proposed house site. I would sit there and draw house plans while Doug wandered to see what plants he could find. Then I would go over to the edge of the forest and just absorb everything.

> I felt deep peace and contentment, which I had never felt before.

I cried again as I watched Doug wandering around the forest. I thought of him as the horse, and I also watched his comfortable connection with the natural world.

I felt so fortunate. It was almost three years since I had been crying in the corner of my bedroom. With the help of my amazing psychologist Jannelle, and the power of writing to my child self and my best friend God, I had managed to find the right path.

I had experienced every emotion, I'd had a marriage crisis, I had bought a horse, I had enhanced my sixth sense and communicated with the invisible world – and now I had found the horse I had been searching for. Together we

had found the farm. I felt deep peace and contentment, which I had never felt before.

I knew there was so much more to this journey, but in that moment, I felt peace. The forest was enveloped in magic and I felt protected, inspired and content.

I was finally home in my place of living and I was now on the right path to feeling at home with myself. That would take much more work and, as I have found, is an ongoing process.

At that time, I had no idea I was about to embark on another journey, with the arrival of the horses. I will tell you that special story in my next book.

Just remember – there is nothing to fear!

•●•

TWELVE TOP TIPS

YOU ARE NOT ALONE

SLEEP IS A WONDERFUL HEALER

UNCONDITIONAL LOVE EQUALS EMPOWERMENT

AS YOUR FALSE SELF DROPS AWAY, YOUR FALSE FRIENDS WILL TOO

EXPLORE YOUR LONGINGS

WRITING IS HEALING

DO NOT BOTTLE UP GRIEF – LET IT OUT!

EVERYONE HAS POTENTIAL

TIME IS NEEDED TO SORT OUT CHANGES IN A RELATIONSHIP

ENJOY THE QUIET – YOU WILL HEAR SO MUCH!

START WRITING – ANYTHING! SEE WHERE IT LEADS!

TAKE THAT LEAP – IT WILL ALL BE OKAY!

Afterword

Research into depression has come a long way since my breakdown in 2000. It is now accepted as a serious condition, not just something to 'soldier on' with. There is also new research on the effects of a mother's postnatal depression on their baby. I recommend reading *Scared Sick* by Robin Karr-Morse.

I'm a firm believer in professional help – not only with counselling, but with medication. There are times when you may be so far down in the pit of depression and anxiety that you need medication to function. I suggest you do whatever helps you. There are no rules and no shame. Just don't suffer in silence!

For me it was important to trace my history. I wanted to know why I had felt like that – where it had come from. The Study of Myself gave me an awareness of developmental stages that were missed. I could see why I had the thoughts I did. It enabled me to grieve what I hadn't grieved and to gain a new and improved view of myself and the world around me.

However, this is just a start. This work is not an instant cure – it requires constant monitoring and it is easy to slip back into lifelong habits. I still work at it, but I have come so far since that time.

Thank you for taking time to read my story. My hope is that it will inspire you in some way, whether to seek help for a troubled soul or to find your burning passion within.

I will be creating a series of books under the umbrella of *Horse Magic Stories*. This name was born from all that the horses have taught me and the stories they have shared.

My next book is called *The Promise*. You will learn what happened after our move, the ups and downs, and the ongoing revelations I had. The horses started arriving and brought their own stories with them. They became my most important teachers as I embarked on the biggest challenge of my life. I sometimes despaired, but then I would hear that quiet whisper, that voice of reason and encouragement that lies within, and it gave me the strength to carry on, when sometimes all seemed hopeless.

In *The Promise* I will be sharing ways you too can overcome your own challenges. Remember, There Is Nothing To Fear!

Take care,

About The Author

Heather is the middle child, born in 1956, to parents Richard and Betty. She has an older sister, Ros, and a younger sister, Sue. About 15 years ago, she discovered she has a half-sister, Liz!

Heather lives in Australia and spent her early childhood in Sydney, before moving to Tamworth for several years. It was here that she had her first taste of country life which she loved. However, after family tragedy, she found herself in Sydney again. She once again escaped Sydney life in her late teens and moved to the far north coast of NSW. Again, with young children, she found herself in Sydney, but finally escaped its clutches 25 years ago.

Since then, she has lived in the Coffs Harbour area and now enjoys each day living on 100 acres with her husband, Doug, her four horses, Magnum, Ducati, Danny and Saadi, and her ragdoll cat, Roger.

Heather has two adult children, Matt and Emma, who are happily settled in life with their partners.

Heather has had a varied career, starting in administrative work, before she moved to her most important career – a full-time mother. During this time, she became a Nursing Mothers' counsellor, and enjoyed facilitating groups for new mothers, as well as working part time in administration.

In the last 25 years she has organised a community group called Adventure Girls, studied for a social science degree, and studied horse management. She also developed her psychic abilities and opened a business with her friend, Sheryl. Together they ran group courses in psychic development, finding your purpose and meditation.

About twelve years ago she became interested in transcendental meditation TM® and began hosting classes at her property. She practises TM® most days and it has enhanced her peacefulness.

Her psychic work led to animal communication, and she now specialises in horses, which are her passion. She also trains her own horses using positive reinforcement and writes a blog on her adventures.

About The Author

In the future she will be writing more books and developing more projects while following her passions.

Her two mantras:

THERE IS NOTHING TO FEAR

YOU ARE NEVER TOO OLD!

Website:
www.horsemagicstories.com

Contact:
horsemagicstories@gmail.com

YouTube Channel:
https://tinyurl.com/horsemagicmedia

Book Reviews From The Family

'A great reflection on what is truly important in life, how to face trauma, and how negativity and fear can undermine not only your own life, but the lives of those around you. Well done Mum, I'm eager to read the next one!'

Dr. Matthew Binns

'Engaging and well-written. So proud of Mum for sharing her experiences. I am grateful to have such amazing parents.'

**Emma Binns,
Perioperative RN**

'So proud of my sister, Heather, for not only finally writing this book but going through the very brave journey from breakdown to enlightenment.

To read her descriptions of the childhood I shared, and what our family was like, was very enlightening for me. I remember some very good times, but Heather's writings made me realise that there were many things sadly lacking in our upbringing, such as affection and support when we needed it. I now understand much better why I am the person that I am. In particular, the chapter on our Dad's early death and how this was handled made me realise what a big impact this has had on my development.

This book will definitely resonate with anyone wanting to find their true self or their passion in life. It is an engaging read and the learnings and tips at the end of each chapter are invaluable.'

Sue Usher, Sister

'Heather has put her heart and soul into this book and I'm extremely proud of her achievement. For someone who has lived the first 20 years or so with her, it is quite strange – and uncomfortable at times – to read about yourself and your family through someone else's eyes. But it has helped me to rationalise some long-standing issues, particularly around our father's early death, and the guilt I felt about leaving Australia in the 1980s to travel and ultimately establish a new life and career in the UK. I am sure all readers will find something in Heather's book that they can relate to and learn from. As she says…there is nothing to fear!'

Ros Crawford, Sister

Heather Binns

Heather Binns, the author of *There Is Nothing To Fear*, is an engaging speaker who easily connects with the audience in several fun exercises to get them started on the life adventure they have dreamed of.

Heather has adopted the mantra, 'There is Nothing to Fear', as a result of her breakdown 20 years ago, which led to her finding her real self and long buried passion. The experience introduced her to the unseen world and connectedness of everything.

Heather was the founder of a fun group for women called Adventure Girls, has taught courses in psychic development and finding your purpose, and is an animal communicator with her focus on horses. She practises transcendental meditation TM® daily.

These passions have led Heather to a framework that can transform the lives of those that feel stuck, unfulfilled, and posing the big life question: Is this all there is?

Here are Heather's three most requested presentations and she can also customise any presentation to any audience.

IS THIS ALL THERE IS IN LIFE?

- Have you reached a crossroad in life? Heather's story will help you navigate your way forward.
- What's wrong with me? Recognising the symptoms of inner turmoil.
- Don't ignore the signs – they will get louder!

EMBRACING CHANGE WITHOUT FEAR

- What will I do now? When to get expert help.
- Pressure to conform – stepping away from outside expectations.
- Mindset – building the confidence to change

SEARCHING FOR YOURSELF – TOOLS FOR DISCOVERY

- Meditation – a relaxed body and mind can hear so much better!
- Journaling – the power of automatic writing!
- Let's take a card - learning to develop your sixth sense!

CONTACT

- www.horsemagicstories.com
- horsemagicstories@gmail.com
- 0438 537 405

horse magic stories

...a place of kindness

fun and adventure

Acknowledgements

- A huge thanks to Jannelle Geraghty, my counsellor and guide throughout my therapy.

- Special thanks to Doug, for reading through my manuscript several times and helping me with writing style. Thanks also for all the chores you have taken on during my writing. I truly appreciate it and love you heaps!

- To my sister, Sue - thanks for being my sounding board and helping me with so many aspects of book writing!

- Thanks also to my sister, Ros for your editing input and family history details!

- Thanks to my children, Matt and Emma, and their partners, Isobel and Max, for your continued support!

- To my good friend, Sheryl – thanks so much for your outstanding support and guided meditations to help me through.

- To the Ultimate 48 Hour Author Team – thank you for your support!

- Thanks so much to Yelena Fishman, my fellow author, who has been a wonderful friend and source of support throughout this journey.

- And last but not least – to my horses – Ducati, Magnum, Danny and Saadi – thank you for providing much needed grounding and relaxation during the writing frenzy!

Notes

www.ingramcontent.com/pod-product-compliance
Lightning Source LLC
Chambersburg PA
CBHW071729080526
44588CB00013B/1949